Joan Clarke
The Biography of a Bletchley Park Enigma

By the author of

Jack the Ripper – Blood Lines
and
Edith Cavell – Brussels via Yorc

Joan Clarke

The Biography of a Bletchley Park Enigma

The life of Joan Clarke; her work at Bletchley Park, her lost ten years
in Scotland, and a life spent in the shadows

Anthony J Randall

First published in the United Kingdom in 2019 by
The Cloister House Press

ISBN 978-1-909465-96-1

FOREWORD

When first beginning to study the wartime work at Bletchley Park, one of the most unexpected aspects that came to light was that the breaking of *Enigma* was not simply an exercise in mathematics. What was important was the mind and intellect of the codebreaker, be they a mathematician, a classics scholar, a historian, a language expert or a chess champion. In Alan Turing, GC&CS at Bletchley Park found a mathematical mind of epic proportions. In Joan Clarke, they found a mathematician whose ability, destined to forever lie within his shadow, would stay with the task of attacking the German U-Boat threat for the entire course of the war.

But there was more to Joan Clarke than was demonstrated by her time at Bletchley Park during the war. Her success made her value to GCHQ such that she served long beyond what should have been her expected retirement age for a woman, even beyond the expected age for a man, taking on a consultancy role after her sixty-fifth birthday.

For ten years she was lost to history; lost in Scotland; what she was doing during those Cold War years is not recorded – falling off the radar. After her sojourn in Fife, in the midst of the intelligence war against Soviet Russia, she took up the reins again, working with old colleagues from Bletchley Park, and Eastcote.

She had interests outside GCHQ, interests that brought her the recognition that her day job would not allow. Her attention to detail, combined with her analytical skills, made her an expert in the field of numismatics as it had in the field of military intelligence.

Coming from a family that was firmly rooted in the Anglican Church, her faith stayed with her all her life. Not in an overt manner, but giving her an underlying peace and composure; her death came quietly and without pain, her funeral being a quiet family affair, both events understating the enormous contribution she made to her country.

This book is not intended to be about *Enigma*, nor how *Enigma* was broken, but it is about a woman who made a contribution to the breaking of *Enigma* and, after that, to the defence of the Western World.

Anthony J Randall

Sheringham, Norfolk

CONTENTS

ACKNOWLEDGEMENTS

Katherine Walker and Alec Coutts - New Forest Heritage Centre

Sue Bradman, Jonathan and Helen Armitage - Crail Museum

Diane Blackett - Filkins

Philip A Crawford – International Probate, Estepona, Spain

Pat Goodland – London, Ontario

Derek and Richard Leppard – Uckington

Anne Robertson – Crail

Andrew Hodges - Oxford

Family: William Clarke - Sheffield

                  John Clarke – Maidenhead

                  Christine Laignel – Jersey, CI

Thanks also to my wife Isabel who has been my sounding board for many months and has travelled with me to various parts of the country so that I might pursue my interest in this remarkable woman. We have enjoyed our time in Chichester and in the New Forest and have visited Bletchley Park on numerous occasions. My thanks also go to GCHQ for sending Joan to Fife; the memory of our time spent in the beautiful town of Crail, and the friendliness of the people we met, will stay with us forever.

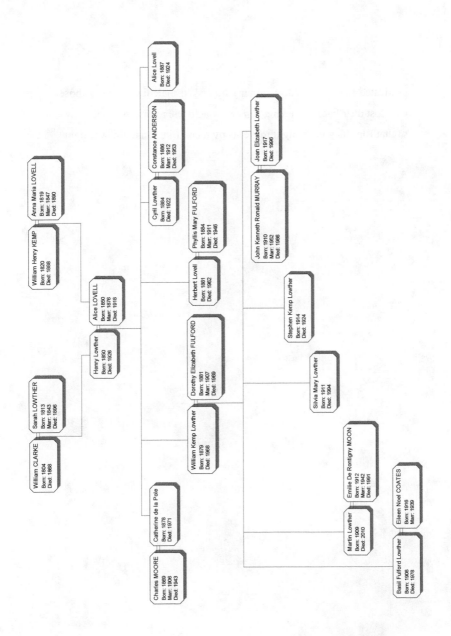

Dedicated to the men and women who risked their lives, and to those who lost their lives, retrieving *Enigma* machines, rotors and code books so that Bletchley Park might make its own contribution to the war fight.

CHAPTER 1

LAMBETH CONFERENCE

Passing the North Foreland to port, the eleven thousand ton TSS *Themistocles* changed course to steer due west as it entered the outer reaches of the Thames Estuary. For most of the previous twelve hours the ship had been steaming east and then, once through the Dover Straits, north. On the previous evening, Wednesday 28th April 1920, she had left Plymouth bound for London and now, as the first-class passengers took breakfast in the main deck restaurant, they were anticipating the end of their twelve-thousand mile voyage from Brisbane; the fore-noon would be spent in surveying the North Kent shore-line before partaking of a final light lunch, and exchanging farewells with Captain Jermyn and his officers.

One hundred first-class passengers occupied the prime cabins and staterooms, and were able to enjoy the library and the two first-class lounges, the smoking room, and a 'delightful veranda café' on the aft deck. However, *Themistocles* also carried two hundred and fifty third-class passengers, more constrained in their freedom aboard ship, but comfortably accommodated and well catered for during their forty-day journey. For a number of passengers, Plymouth had been their final destination, with a few completing their journey a day or so earlier in Tenerife. In the last few hours of sailing, third class passengers were busy packing; first-class passengers were content to delegate that task to their stewards.

Among the first-class passengers were a father and daughter who had boarded *Themistocles* in Melbourne and were now returning to Britain, from whence they had departed eighteen years previously. Henry Lowther Clarke had not seen his son, William for some years, nor had he yet met William's wife Dorothy, or their five children. With Henry was his youngest daughter Alice, now thirty-three years old, but not married; she had nursed her mother through her dying months and was now returning to visit her brothers William and Herbert, and her elder sister Catherine. Her other brother, Dr. Cyril Lowther Clarke, had stayed on to tend his medical practice in South Australia.

1

The ship passed by the Isle of Sheppey to the south and entered the River Thames, the southern shore of Essex on the starboard side, becoming clearer as the channel narrowed and then turned suddenly south, before approaching Gravesend to port and Tilbury to starboard. The entrance to Tilbury docks was through a narrow 'cut' approached from the west, which necessitated *Themistocles* making a 180^0 turn in the narrow river. As the engines were stopped *Themistocles* was approached by three tugs, took on lines, and allowed herself to be maneuvered through the narrow entrance and into her berth.

Meanwhile, at 193 Rosendale Road in Dulwich, the household was busily preparing for its visitors. The Reverend William Kemp Lowther Clarke held the living at All Saints' Church in West Dulwich and was preparing to welcome his father Henry and sister Alice to his new home and his new parish. The five bedroom house, opposite open fields, was suitably large enough for a 'man of the cloth' and, although he no longer had resident servants as at his previous country parishes, his home life echoed the conservative nature of his calling, of his politics and of his family background.

> *AUTHOR'S NOTE: All Saints Church, West Dulwich, was built in the last few years of the nineteenth century of brick with a stone dressing. The original design, by George Fellowes Prynne, was for a larger church but truncated with three bays less than planned. In June 1944 a V1 flying bomb exploded near the church, at the junction of Rosendale and Lovelace Roads, killing at least four people, damaging the roof and shattering the stained glass windows. William Clarke, Joan's father, not yet moved to Chichester, continued to hold services, but in the crypt. In 2000 the interior was destroyed by fire, restoration being complete by 2006.*

The Reverend William Clarke arrived at Tilbury Docks to see *Themistocles* being turned ready to enter the narrow 'cut' that led to her allocated berth. As she turned on her axis under the strain of the tugs, the silhouette of her two masts, remnants of a bygone sailing age, penetrated the sky. Mid-ships the single orange funnel, dwarfed by her two masts, let out a thin wisp of smoke, signifying engines at standby, powering only the essential domestic services. Gently, the ship edged its way slowly forward and into the Tilbury Docks, the decks lined with passengers, the majority straining to see welcoming faces there to greet them.

Final berthing of the liner was accompanied by the usual inexplicable frustrations of such enterprises. Lines ashore secured, gangplanks lowered for port authorities and customs officers to board, paperwork to be signed and, finally, walkways for passengers to progress ashore. The first-class walkways were the first to be opened, with a few passengers seeking to avoid the inevitable queues at immigration and customs, their luggage being carried ashore by stewards. Less frenetic departures were enjoyed by those for whom business and trade was not the driving force. Third-class passengers were then able to make their way down the other walkways and into the customs hall, where their luggage was to be reclaimed from the general repository.

Henry Clarke was dressed, unmistakably, in clerical attire; his black serge suit, formal top hat, and white clerical collar surmounting his black plain fronted shirt. Had he not spent the previous few years in Australia, he may well have adopted the knee breeches and morning coat as worn by his British counterparts. Doctor the Very Reverend Henry Lowther Clark, Archbishop of Melbourne, had come to London to attend the sixth Lambeth Conference to be presided over by Randall Thomas Davidson, Archbishop of Canterbury. The time for formal attire would come once the conference began, for the time being he was simply a father and grandfather returning to England following the loss of his wife after forty-four years of marriage.

The Archbishop of Melbourne and his daughter emerged from the customs hall to encounter a throng of faces. The clerical collar of his son, William, caught his eye instantly and the two shook one another's hand. William removed his hat and bent down to embrace his sister Alice, eight years his junior. The porter, with luggage from the voyage, had already engaged a taxi for the journey to Dulwich and, having been tipped handsomely, left his charges to complete their journey. A taxi was something of an extravagance for William, but was quite justified for an Archbishop on church business. In 1920, the most easterly Thames crossing point was the Blackwall Tunnel, which took them through Greenwich and then home to Dulwich.

As the taxi drew up outside 193 Rosendale Road a small reception committee assembled on the footpath. The Archbishop settled with the driver before disembarking with Alice, the luggage being disgorged onto the pavement under the supervision of his son William. This was the first occasion on which William had been able to introduce the family to his father and youngest sister. First there was his wife Dorothy, followed by their five children, Basil aged twelve, Martin, Silvia, Stephen and finally their youngest, Joan just coming up for three years old. There had, of course, been exchanges of letters and photographs, but this was the first time they had all come together as a family.

Joan Elisabeth Lowther Clarke at one year old, with her nurse, at Crowmarsh in Hampshire.

(courtesy of Christine Laignel, Joan's niece)

While Henry and Alice were ushered into the house by William and Dorothy, their two sons were charged with bringing the luggage into the house and then, with their father's assistance, taking it up to the two bedrooms allocated to their visitors. For the duration of the visit the three boys were to share the one room, Silvia and Joan would share the other. The Lambeth Conference was not due to open until August, but Henry and Alice were intending to spend only part of their allotted time in England with William and his family; they had other relatives to visit and Henry needed time to prepare for the conference. The disturbed living arrangements in Rosendale Road would be of finite duration.

As the family sat down together for afternoon tea, the children were each able to present themselves to their grandfather and aunt. As in all such gatherings the youngest, especially being a girl, assumes command of the assembled visitors and Joan Elisabeth Lowther Clarke, aged "two years, ten months and five days" was keen to demonstrate her prowess in both her numbers and letters, although the latter was confined to illustrated bible stories, in keeping with her father's calling. Her grandfather approved these early signs of academic endeavor and also that 'Lowther', being his own mother's maiden name, was being continued through to a further generation; it was a testament to tradition that all William's children carried that name.

While the children were being put to bed by Dorothy and Alice, the two men had an opportunity to talk, particularly about the passing of William's mother in 1918. The death of Alice had led Henry to consider what the future in Australia could offer. Four of his five children, if he included his daughter Alice, were now in England; his son Cyril was living six hundred miles from his home in Melbourne and, if Henry were to return to Australia, he may never see his English grandchildren again. He was sixty-nine years old and he had given his closest advisors in Melbourne warning of his plan to announce his retirement immediately prior to his seventieth birthday, which fell on the 23rd November, shortly after the Lambeth Conference.

In the days that followed, Henry and his daughter sought, and were given, an opportunity to recover from their long and arduous journey. In Australia they had led simple lives, despite Henry's rank within the Church, travelling by train or tram and carrying his robes and vestments in a basket suitcase. He had visited aboriginal stations and settlement towns and had played his part in preaching Christianity to the indigenous population but he was not convinced that an intellectual and spiritual transformation was possible to achieve. That summer's Lambeth Conference, with its emphasis on opposing the use of artificial contraception, was at odds with Henry's experience among the aboriginals and poor whites of Australia.

Attending Sunday service at All Saints' Church, his son was able to introduce Henry as something of a celebrity. He was tall and handsome but, beneath a rather blunt north-country manner he concealed considerable shyness and tenderness; he enjoyed a joke against himself and, with family and intimates, he revealed a softer, even sentimental, side to his nature. The Archbishop of Melbourne was a witty and lively conversationalist, interested in music and the fine arts, and well read in the poets; he was a clear, scholarly and forcible speaker, and his contribution to the day was received with praise and appreciation.

Alice was anxious to see her elder sister Catherine, who had married Charles Moore, a chaplain in the Royal Navy, and was living in Greenwich with their two children, Elizabeth and Henry. Catherine had been born 1877, while her father was curate at St John's Church in Kingston-on-Hull. The naming of his first child was a reflection of Henry's enthusiasm for his calling and for the town in which he first held office; his decision was to name her after the Abbess of Barking Abbey, who was born in Kingston-on-Hull in the fifteenth century. Catherine de la Pole Clarke was duly baptised into the Church of England but then dropped the 'de la Pole' on every occasion that she was able. Catherine had moved to Australia with her father and mother but had travelled back to Britain in 1906 to be married.

This was the first time that Catherine and her father had met since her mother's death. Alice had been the nurse during the brief illness but Catherine, excluded by reason of distance, had not been able to share her grief in communion with her father, but only to express her feelings by letter. Alice had been a girl of eighteen when she and Catherine last talked as sisters and was, only now, able to express the concerns over their father's health and to voice her worry that he might go back on his resolve to retire from his position within the Church and, instead, resume his arduous duties. Alice's own health was not good and, should her father's health deteriorate further, would feel isolated back in Australia. The two sisters resolved that this could not be allowed to happen.

The older children, from both families, were all at school leaving only Joan to sit and listen to the 'grown-ups'. This was the pattern for much of the time that Rosendale Road was playing host to her grandfather and aunt. William and his father, when

William's duties would permit, spent much time discussing the academic work on which each was engaged. Joan was a constant companion to her grandfather, absorbing the atmosphere of study and learning which was ever present within the Clarke family. St. John's College, Cambridge had been the 'alma mater' of Henry and of his two sons. Henry, while resident in Melbourne, had published a number of works through English publishers and expressed his intention to continue his studies during his planned retirement.

The Reverend Herbert Lovell Clarke was the Vicar of All Saints' Church in Nottingham and had been since just before the First World War, during which he had served for a short period with the Sherwood Foresters. He and his father had not seen each other for many years and a visit to Nottingham was high on Henry's priority list. It was not practical for Herbert, his wife and five children, to journey to London so it was decided that Henry and Alice would take the train to Nottingham; they would be accompanied by William's wife Dorothy and youngest child, Joan, who was not yet attending school.

Dorothy Elizabeth Fulford had married William Clarke in 1907; her sister Phyllis Mary Fulford had married William's brother, Herbert, four years later. Whereas the brothers would have had opportunities, through their involvement in the Church, to meet from time to time, the two sisters rarely had such an opportunity; such a family visit was a chance not to be missed. Herbert and Phyllis also had a young daughter under school age, Margaret; she and Joan would be companions for one another during the visit. William would stay behind in Dulwich and take care of the children with temporary daily help.

Railway travel was the most convenient, direct from London's Marylebone station to Nottingham Victoria, depositing Henry and his family within half a mile from All Saints' Church and vicarage. For young Joan this would be the first time she had travelled by train, and an awesome experience it was for such a young child. A railway platform in 1920 was a noisy and dirty place; railway engines were large and smelly, belching smoke and releasing steam, with large driving wheels, track rods and pistons being very evident and, to a small child, just a little frightening. Who better to hold her hand, and introduce her to scientific theory transformed into reality, than a grandfather?

Arriving in Nottingham, the family was met by Herbert and transported by taxi to the All Saints' vicarage where they were introduced to Herbert's wife Phyllis and to their two youngest children. While Herbert and his father were enjoying being reunited after many years, the two sisters were catching up and helping Denis and Margaret, Phyllis' children, to get to know Joan. The other three children returned from school to complete the family and each were introduced to their grandfather and aunt, and to their cousin Joan, for the first time. All Saints' vicarage was very large and three bedrooms were easily found for the guests.

For the two clergymen (father and son) Alice's death in Australia was a matter of reminiscences and soul-searching. Henry's attendance at the forthcoming Lambeth Conference and his planned retirement were discussed at length, as was his daughter's general health and his need to create a role as housekeeper and companion, thus providing her with a home. Herbert's future plans were as uncertain as William's; the Church of England could, and did, move their incumbents from parish to parish with little choice. Where Henry and Alice would settle in England would have to be a decision taken without special regard to where either of the two sons, or daughter, were living. Both the Church and the military were prone to forcing relocation on their members.

> AUTHOR'S NOTE: When the church was built in the gothic style, during the middle of the nineteenth century, All Saints was a wealthy suburb outside the old city boundary but, with the expansion of the city, the parish became an inner-city area of Nottingham and began to suffer some decline following the first war.

At the end of their Nottingham visit, the family returned to Rosendale Road and the family home. Joan went back to her lessons but not yet being of school age, she was still taught by her mother. The minimum school age was set at five years old as a provision of the 1870 Elementary Education Act and this continued to be the generally accepted age at which formal school attendance began. Joan's lessons were informal, and driven by the child's naturel desire to learn rather than her mother's zeal and so it was that her education progressed.

Henry Lowther Clarke, Archbishop of Melbourne
(Courtesy of William Clarke, Joan's nephew)

With the impending start of the Lambeth Conference the attention of Henry, and his counterparts from all over the Anglican world, was turning to the agenda of resolutions to be discussed, and the decisions to be made. While Alice remained in Dulwich, her father decamped to a hotel closer to Lambeth Palace, where he could meet with, and discuss issues with, his fellow delegates. There were receptions to attend, special interest groups to join, arms to be twisted and favours to be called in. Henry's plans for retirement, particularly his financial plans, could depend upon the contacts and relationships that were established during the preamble to the Conference.

The Sixth Lambeth Conference opened on 5th July 1920 at Lambeth Palace in London. Henry Lowther Clarke was at odds with Randall Davidson, Archbishop of Canterbury, who was reluctant to commit to an opinion on the issue of Australian Church autonomy, a cause that Henry supported. He and Davidson had been writing to one another on the subject for the previous three years but much to Henry's chagrin, the Archbishop of Canterbury had avoided giving an opinion[1]. The question put to Davidson was whether the Church of England in Australia would still be bound, legally, by the laws of the Church in England; and would such a move jeopardise the status of the church in Australia[2].

The conference ended without directly addressing the issue and Henry Lowther Clarke kept to his resolve of retiring from office and settling in England, close to the majority of his family. He set about looking for a suitable house, in which to live out his remaining years, and one which offered the space and tranquility to continue his academic pursuits, yet from which he was easily able to access London.

CHAPTER 2

LYMINGTON IN THE NEW FOREST

The following year, 1921, Henry and Alice took up residence at Lymington in the New Forest, overlooking the Lymington River and the Solent. In actual fact, *The Lodge* was just across the river at Walhampton in the parish of Boldre, but Lymington was the main centre of population. The house was convenient to the railway station, journey time to London being about two hours, and close to the pier from where ferries to and from the Isle of Wight departed and arrived. The house had previously been owned by the poet, Coventry Patmore and his third wife Harriet Robson, but had been sold at auction in 1890, five years before his death.

> *AUTHOR'S NOTE: Coventry Patmore lived at The Lodge, with his third wife Harriett, from 1891 to 1896. On his death he was buried in Lymington cemetery, in a section reserved for Roman Catholics. His writings were very few during his years in Lymington, the most notable being his 'Religio Poetae' essays and his book of poetry 'Rod, Root, and Flower'.*

The auction particulars of 1890, prepared by Lewis & Badcock, provide an excellent description of the house and grounds. There were seven 'best' bedrooms, and two dressing rooms, plus a further five bedrooms for servants; two drawing rooms, a dining room, smoking room, study and library; school room, housekeeper's room, butler's room, servants' hall as well as kitchen, scullery, larder and dairy. The three-story house had one principal and two secondary staircases and boasted three bathrooms with toilets. The house also included a basement and wine cellar. The grounds extended to a little over two and a half acres, lawned and with mature trees, an orchard and a kitchen garden.

Henry Clarke immediately changed the name of his house to *Melbourne Lodge*, in recognition of his time in Australia, father and daughter settling down to life in England. London family members were only two hours away and Herbert Clarke, in Nottingham, a further two hours. The spring weather was welcome, they being used to the Australian climate, but rainfall began to fall noticeably below average from February of that year and, as the heat of summer began to take effect, conditions in the south of England became quite unpleasant. Fortunately Henry and Alice's new home was close to the sea, with its cooling influence; Joan and her family in Dulwich were not so lucky but family trips to Lymington and the seaside were more than welcome.

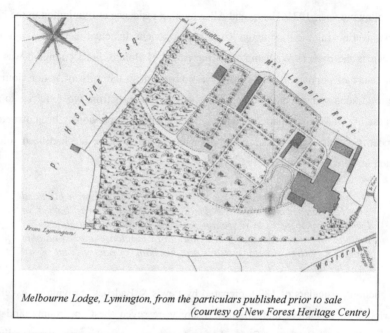

Melbourne Lodge, Lymington, from the particulars published prior to sale
(courtesy of New Forest Heritage Centre)

West Dulwich and the rest of southeast England, was unprepared for the very dry summer of 1921. Open green spaces were turned into a parched yellow landscape and, with less than one quarter of the normal rainfall, fires often broke out. Particularly at risk were the railway embankments, falling easy prey to the sparks and red-hot smuts from steam trains. Botanical gardens, especially Kew Gardens, were severely damaged; the Royal Botanic Gardens bulletin claiming that the thin poor soil was ill adapted to cope with the conditions. Kew claimed that in one period they recorded temperatures in excess of 85°F on eight days, and in excess of 85°F on three days.

The drought and heat wave continued through the summer and into the autumn months. Even in September temperatures as high as 86°F were recorded in the southeast of England and rainfall in some parts increased to only half of that normally expected. In

London the Metropolitan Water Board imposed water restrictions and there was at least one successful prosecution for wasteful water use while washing a car.

Laurie Lee recalled the drought of 1921 in his book *Cider with Rosie*:

> In the long hot summer of 1921 a serious drought hit the country. Springs dried up, the wells filled with frogs, and the usually sweet water from our scullery pump turned brown and tasted of nails. Although this drought was a relief to my family, it was a scourge to the rest of the village. For weeks the sky hung hot and blue, trees shriveled, crops burned in the fields, and old folk said the sun had slipped in its course and that we should all of us very soon die. There were prayers for rain; but my family didn't go, because it was rain we feared most of all[3].

Melbourne Lodge offered Joan, and her brothers and sister, much to distract them; there were visits to the beach, to the forest, to the seawater swimming baths, and to the shops and cafés of Lymington town centre. Visits to Lymington, across the toll bridge, were by pony and trap; further afield they were by train. Of all the activities that would appeal to five urban children, a trip on the paddle steamer *Solent* for a day's outing to the Isle of Wight, was a favourite. In such a hot and dry summer a sea breeze was highly prized.

> The boys in sailor suits with large straw hats . . . The girls usually wore smocks, which they tucked inside their bloomers when paddling, thus providing a curiously balloon like profile. Both sexes carried spades, those of the boys had iron blades which made a splendid crisp indentation in the sand, but the spades of their sisters would have been of wood . . . About the buckets there was little to choose. They were brightly coloured, of tin, and bearing in gold the names of the place of origin until, a summer's hard usage had deleted it[4].

Lymington Toll Bridge c.1921

(acknowledgement to www.lymington.org)

Back in Dulwich, less than two miles from Joan's home in Rosendale Road, a child was born to Fredrick and Lily Lever, another girl who was also destined to make a significant contribution to the war effort in the field of cryptanalysis. Fredrick and Lily Lever occupied a place in a different social stratum than did William and Dorothy Clarke; Frederick was a postman, William a 'clerk in holy orders'. Mavis Lilian Lever, was born 5th May 1921 at 20 Crebor Street in Dulwich; she was eventually to work at Bletchley Park and then, after the war, at Eastcote.

The hot and dry conditions were not confined to Britain, but were experienced in the whole of Western Europe, particularly in France and Germany.

During the early months of 1922 Joan's father, William, published two works through the Society for Promoting Christian Knowledge (SPCK), which had its own network of bookshops and distributers in both Britain and throughout the world. The first was *Evensong Explained* and the second *A Life of Our Saviour for Little Children*, both factual and entirely without emotional content. Such was William's style of writing; analytical, insightful and without flourish, an approach to study that he had learnt from his father and tried to instill in his own children. He had previously had three works published by the society; *The Life of St. Macrina*, *The Lausiac History of Palladius* and *A Short History of the SPCK*; all the result of studious research and completely removed from dogma or theology. His first ever work, a dissertation on monastic life titled *St. Basil the Great*, had given him his Bachelor of Divinity, and been subsequently published by Cambridge University Press in 1913.

> *AUTHOR'S NOTE: The Society for Promoting Christian Knowledge had its origins in the last few years of the seventeenth century to find ways if promoting the understanding of Anglican Christianity through education. This was achieved by the founding of schools and libraries in rural areas. During the nineteenth century the society funded the establishment of schools, libraries and churches overseas, particularly in those countries that were part of the British Empire. From its early beginnings, the society had commissioned tracts and pamphlets that it published and distributed through supporters but later opened its own bookshops.*

While life in England was passing peacefully, with Henry and his daughter settled in Lymington, the family was to be again plunged into despair. It had been only three years since the death of Henry's wife Alice, which had prompted him and his daughter's return to England. They had left Henry's son Cyril behind in Australia, with a wife and two sons and with his medical practice thriving, family and career was set to prosper on the other side of the world. His wife Constance was expecting their third child and the future was looking bright for the Clarke family. As well as having a successful practice, he had been appointed Medical Officer of Health for the Corporation of Peterborough. In 1920 he had been Chairman of Finance of the Municipal Council in 1920 and as Mayor of Peterborough the following year.

Dr. Cyril Lowther Clarke, thirty-eight years old and having survived the First World War, was killed in a motoring accident on 23rd September 1922. Taking a day off from tending to the sick, he had been to the racecourse with friends and, while driving back to his home in Peterborough that evening, one of his rear wheels simply collapsed, causing his car to mount the kerb and then somersault. Cyril and a young passenger were trapped underneath the car and, although being taken to hospital, both died of their injuries.

> The residents in this town and district were shocked to hear last evening that Dr. Cyril Lowther Clarke (Mayor of Peterborough) and Master Frank Cave had been killed, and that three lads . . . had been injured in

a motor accident. The doctor, who was a true sport in every sense of the word, and a great supporter of the local and surrounding race clubs, had attended the Peterborough Races, and he left the course at 5.50 o'clock in his motor car to drive to his home. As he was proceeding along the Main street and was passing another car the right hand hind wheel of his machine collapsed. The car swerved into the gutter, and struck the kerbing. He stuck to the steering wheel, and succeeded in getting the machine almost to the centre of the road again. Then it turned a double somersault backwards. Dr. Clarke fell underneath the car. Young Cave was hurled against the kerbing, and the other lads were thrown on to the footpath. . . hurriedly taken to the Hospital. Neither Mr. Clarke nor Master Cave rallied, and both passed away during the early hours of Sunday morning.

The community is in mourning over the fearful occurrence. Every resident regards the death of the doctor as a great loss. He was a cool, level-headed man, and most temperate, and was one of the finest motor car drivers in the north. He had never been found wanting in the most arduous and extreme cases, and he was beloved by every one. When it was learned on Saturday night that his condition was so serious the picture show and other amusements closed, and the streets and the hospital grounds were crowded by people waiting anxiously for news, and entertaining the hope that the worst would not happen.

Mrs. Clarke had been an inmate of the hospital for several weeks until a few days ago, when she returned home. The sympathy towards her is, therefore, intensified[5].

The news of his son's death reached Henry in Lymington via the telegraphic service from Cyril's wife, Constance, but details were necessarily brief. Letters and telephone calls from Lymington shared the tragic news with Catherine, William and Herbert but it was some weeks later that Constance's letter to her father-in-law arrived. Constance was also able to enclose newspaper cuttings that summarised her husband's life:

His early school days were in Oxford, later at Bedford Grammar School and then he moved to Australia, at the age of eighteen, when his father was appointed the Archbishop of Melbourne. He attended Trinity College and the University of Melbourne, graduating from medicine and surgery with honours in 1908. He settled in Peterborough, SA in April 1911 and was known as a sound practitioner and a person of considerable ability and energy. He married Constance Anderson eldest daughter of the Bishop of Riverina on 14th February 1912 at Hay, New South Wales, his father performing the ceremony.

Clarke joined the Australian Army Medical Corps as a captain in November 1911; enlisted in the Australian Imperial Force in early 1916 and was commissioned as a Major on 1st August 1916. Clarke was diagnosed with malaria during 1918, while in Egypt, and had two relapses returning to duty in June 1919. He was promoted to temporary lieutenant colonel on the 7th March 1919. Clarke had a glowing recommendation from Brigadier General Ryrie, and for a time served as Director of Medical Services with the Australian Mounted Division. He returned to Australia on the *Burma* on the 26th July 1919 with his appointment terminated on the 8th November 1919. He was issued with the British War Medal and the Victory Medal.

As disturbing as the news was for the family, their loss was made even more difficult to bear as Cyril's wife, Constance, was expecting their third child within weeks of losing Cyril. There was a general sense of loss and concern among the family in England, and it was some weeks before news of Nancy Clarke's birth reached Lymington, and thence to Dulwich and Nottingham. For Joan, these events were somewhat separated from the daily life of a five year old; she had never met her uncle Cyril, nor her aunt Constance, and the arrival into this world of a third Australian cousin made very little impact on one whose outlook on life was more factual than fantasy.

In 1923 Joan's uncle and aunt, Herbert and Phyllis Clarke, left Nottingham in order that Herbert could take up a new post in Leeds, as vicar of St Bartholomew, Armley, which also entailed him taking on the role of prison chaplain. This latter obligation was, to say the least, a testing one for him. Armley prison was one that carried out executions more frequently than did others, and one of the prison chaplain's duties was to visit the prisoner and attend the hanging. This unpleasant duty fell to Herbert, not long after taking on the role, when he attended the execution of John Eastwood who had been found guilty of murdering John Joseph Clarke (no relation) in Sheffield.

The Sheffield Daily Telegraph reported:

> At 9 o'clock this morning John William Eastwood (39), until lately the proprietor of the Bay Horse Hotel, Sheffield, was executed at the Armley Gaol, Leeds, for the murder of John Joseph Clarke, who had been employed by him as a barman. Ellis was the executioner and the proceedings were carried out without hitch. Eastwood was transferred from the condemned cell to a smaller cell on Thursday night, and yesterday morning he had only to walk a few steps to the scaffold. It was stated that he had a fair night, but was assisted across to the platform. There were present the Sheriff of the County (colonel FRT Gascoigne), the Governor of the Gaol (Captain AC Scott), the Acting Under-Sheriff (Mr B Dodsworth), and the Chaplain.

The process was, in fact, more onerous than walking a few steps with the condemned man. Armley Gaol, like Newgate, Wandsworth, Warwick and Strangeways had execution sheds built in one of their exercise yards to house the gallows. The shed stood apart from the main buildings and necessitated a fairly lengthy walk from the condemned cell to the shed where he trapdoors were typically installed over a brick lined pit. Having the gallows in a separate building spared other prisoners from the sound of the trap falling and made it easier for staff to deal with the execution and removal of the body afterwards. This was too much for Herbert Clarke and, following the execution, resigned his post as Prison Chaplain but continued as Vicar of Armley.

Basil Clarke, Joan's eldest brother, showed an early interest in the fabric of churches, not surprising given the fact that his father, uncles and both grandfathers were, or had all been, members of the Anglican clergy. At fifteen years old, he and his younger brother Martin began to visit churches in their immediate area. London offered a great many churches for study, old and not so old and of many different designs, and the two brothers began to venture further and further in pursuit of their hobby. Their father, William, encouraged his sons' interest and persuaded them of the need to properly document their researches. The Clarke thirst for knowledge and for thorough academic study, was very much in the tradition of the family and the two boys readily embraced their father's wishes.

AUTHOR'S NOTE: Basil Clarke's partnership with his brother Martin continued until 1932, after which he continued to work alone. Over the course of some fifty-five years he visited more than eleven thousand churches (Anglican and Roman Catholic) and filled 31 notebooks with a combination of notes taken from primary and secondary sources as well as his own observations. The archive is held by The Council for the Care of Churches.

Martin and Basil Clarke, Joan's brothers, pictured in 1957
(courtesy of John Clarke, Joan's nephew)

During 1924 Joan was to experience a loss much closer to home than that of her uncle Cyril in Australia, who she had never met. Stephen, Joan's nine-year old brother, had never been a strong child and was thought to have some fundamental weakness in his heart. In early 1924 Stephen contracted measles, not uncommon among children at that time, but one which parents dreaded.

The period of incubation is from seven to fourteen days, and this is followed by a pre-eruptive period lasting about four days, during which time the patient has catarrhal symptoms, chilliness, sneezing, a cough, and running at the eyes and nose. During the pre-eruptive stage characteristic spots, known as Koplik spots, appear on the buccal mucous membrane.

The pre-eruptive period is followed by the characteristic blotchy deep mulberry red macular eruption which starts on the forehead and behind the ears and quickly spreads over the whole body. There is a rapid rise of temperature as the rash comes out, rapid respiration, bronchial catarrh, and congested mucous membranes[6].

Measles, although a common childhood disease, was not a minor illness. In 1924 there were one thousand three hundred and thirty deaths from measles and for Stephen, suffering with a congenital heart disease, the stress upon him was far too much, and he finally succumbed on the 6th March, dying at home with his mother and father to comfort him.

For Joan, her brother's illness was trauma enough for a six-year old girl to bear, but to watch his gradual decline, through the fever, to witness his struggle and to sense the growing desperation of parents and doctors, would have been beyond her understanding. Stephen had been her playmate and her confidante during her early years, now her sister Silvia, at fourteen, had to take on that role. During the latter stages of Stephen's illness, and in the days following his death, her aunt Alice had come up from Lymington to support William and Dorothy and to take care of the younger children. Joan's grandfather, Henry, journeyed from Lymington to attend the funeral and then returned leaving Alice to help her bother and her sister-in-law.

CHAPTER 3

AUNT AND GRANDFATHER

Alice Clarke had taken rooms with a Mrs Gobbett at 30 Hamlet Road in Penge while she spent a little time in the capital. Her eldest sister Catherine was not far away and it was clear that William and Dorothy needed some time with their children. Joan, in particular, was missing her brother and the adult world of funerals was beyond the comprehension of such a young child. Alice was well used to being alone and London held no terrors for her. She could travel by bus and train quite comfortably and cheaply, and an extended stay was to be welcomed before returning to the parochial life of Lymington.

A week after Stephen's funeral Alice began to complain of a fever. The influenza pandemic of a few years earlier meant that the family, and the population at large, knew the signs only too well and were well aware of the complications that could follow such illness, and of the possible outcome. Influenza was soon diagnosed.

> *AUTHOR'S NOTE: Although the influenza pandemic of 1918 (Spanish flu) was largely over shortly after the end of the war, the disease was still widely known in the metropolitan cities. About ten percent of cases resulted in death, mostly by secondary causes affecting the respiratory system, and tended to claim the lives of those who were not in the strongest health.*

Within three days Alice had developed pneumonia and was feared to be in danger of her life. Her father, Henry, journeyed back up to London from Lymington but Alice succumbed to the pneumonia on the twenty-fifth of March. By the twenty-eighth, her body had been moved back to Lymington where she was buried in the Highfield Road cemetery, her father conducting the funeral service in the Church of St Thomas the Apostle. When Alice's affairs were concluded, and probate granted to her father, she left an estate of just under £4,000.

Henry, now alone in Lymington, was left to pursue his studies and to finish the work that he had begun following the Lambeth Conference. Later that year Henry Lowther Clarke's most influential work was published by the Society for Promoting Christian

Knowledge (SPCK) of which his son, William, was the editorial secretary. In his book, *Constitutional Church Government in the Dominions Beyond the Seas*, he tackled the constitutional question as to the degree of independence that the Dominion Churches commanded, or should command. This was a matter of which Henry had some knowledge, and strong opinions, gained from his years in Australia. It had also been the subject of much debate among the Lambeth conference delegates and was feared to be a divisive issue within the world-wide Anglican Church.

On the 18th June 1925 the *SS Euripides* sailed into the Solent, passing The Needles to starboard and the New Forest to port. The Lymington River opened up to view as *Euripides* continued to steam slowly east, past Cowes before making a hard turn to port in order to enter Southampton Water and her final destination. At *Melbourne Lodge* on the banks of the Lymington River, an old man sat in his first floor library and, looking out to sea, watched the *Euripides* pass by in the distance. On board, travelling first-class, was his widowed daughter-in-law, Constance, and her three children David, Cyril and Nancy, who had not even been born when Dr. Cyril Lowther Clarke had been killed in the motoring accident.

Henry Lowther Clarke was not a well man and, on his doctor's advice, was spending more and more time at home; but he was waiting on the quayside when his Australian family stepped ashore, and they all journeyed back to *Melbourne Lodge* in the hired motorcar which had now superseded Henry's horse and trap. His grandchildren, free from the confines of ship-board life, were able to explore the grounds of *Melbourne Lodge* while Henry and Constance renewed the friendship which had developed during the war years when she and David had lived with Henry and his wife at their official residence, *Bishopscourt*, in Melbourne.

> *AUTHOR'S NOTE: Bishopscourt was the official residence of the Anglican Archbishop of Melbourne and was home to Henry Clarke and his family during his years in office, before that it was used as Victoria's Government House. The gardens extend to about two acres and are so beautiful that they are still visited as a tourist attraction.*

Constance and the children did not stay long in Lymington, travelling to London where her sister-in-law Catherine and brother-in-law William were both living. She and Alice had been quite close friends in Australia, although she had lived in South Australia and Alice in Victoria, some six hundred miles distant. Constance's parents were both dead and although she had distant cousins in rural England she was determined to begin a new life for her children in London.

In the summer of 1926, Henry Lowther Clarke, now seventy-five years old, was visiting the village of Filkins in the west of Oxfordshire, staying at The Gray House on the Burford Road. This was home to two sisters, both unmarried, who Henry had known in Australia. The two ladies, each a Miss Rose, had strong family connections with the village; the Rose family had been known there since the early part of the nineteenth century.

The Gray House, Filkins, Gloucestershire

(author's photograph)

The visit to Filkins came after a period of illness at home in Lymington, serious enough for him to have been confined to the house since the previous summer. An old man, he had been spared the summer invasion of the young Clarkes from Dulwich so had experienced a long period of solitude except for his housekeeper and small staff. Enjoying the company of old friends in the Oxfordshire countryside was a fitting end to what had been a cultured life, yet one of frustration with the Anglican establishment and its reluctance to reflect the changing Empire.

So it was, while staying with his old friends, that Henry developed a bronchial infection that then led to pneumonia. His son Herbert travelled down from Armley in Leeds, and was present at the death. Henry's wish had been to be laid to rest with his daughter in Lymington, so his burial was also at the Highfield Road cemetery. As a mark of his position within the Anglican Church his funeral service was conducted by Frank Theodore Woods, the Right Reverend the Lord Bishop of Winchester, who had been a friend of Henry's since serving as Episcopal Secretary for the 1920 Lambeth Conference.

The family again gathered together for the funeral, *Melbourne Lodge* being large enough to accommodate the various families. This was the last time that Joan would visit Lymington before the house was closed up and sold. When probate was granted to his sons, William and Herbert, their father's estate was valued at £18,938, a very significant sum.

St John's College, Cambridge published an obituary in its magazine The Eagle, in December of that year:

> Henry Lowther Clarke was born at Firbank Vicarage in Westmorland on November 23rd, 1850. He was educated at home by his father and, later, at the neighbouring Sedbergh School, then in low water as regards numbers and efficiency. But the old-fashioned classical discipline that he received from his father combined with his private study of mathematics formed intellectual habits that lasted a lifetime. From Sedbergh he went to St John's College, Cambridge, as a Sizar and Exhibitioner, being elected to a Foundation Scholarship after two years. His mother had been left a widow with five children. She took a little house in Cambridge, and on an income that never exceeded £300 a year sent her three sons to the University. What the burden meant to her may be gathered from a letter written to Henry Lowther, to be read after her death: "I hope she [your wife] may not be left with such a charge as I was; the responsibility is heavy. I trusted in God and I have been mercifully dealt with. I have gone to bed many a time half broken and

hysterical, but I put my trust in God, and in the morning I felt a new creature, able to struggle with the coming day's work."

The future Bishop's life was necessarily Spartan. He refused all social invitations, for how could he return them? For St John's he cherished a deep affection. He died just too soon to see his boat after 50 years go Head of the River in the May Races, which would have given him the keenest pleasure. Sedbergh, too, never had a more loyal son; fortunately he lived long enough to write her history.

After taking a high degree, Seventh Wrangler, in 1874, Henry Lowther Clarke was ordained, and served his first curacy in Hull. There he married Alice Lovell Kemp, of whom he said to one of his sons: "I was a raw lad from the North. I had character, intellect, initiative – that was all. Whatever I have of gentleness and manners I learned gradually from your mother." This was an over-statement – the natural refinement of his Northern home with its piety, simplicity, and intellectual interests was considerable – but none the less touching.

After two years in Hull he became Vicar of Hedon, six miles away, a tiny municipal borough with a minster-like church. His life there can be summarised in his own words. "Every afternoon without fail I turned out at 2.30 and visited until 5. There were no services except on Sunday and on Wednesday, when I gave a Bible Reading in church to about 70 people. There were no meetings in the parish, and no clerical gatherings except once a year when the Rural Dean invited us to his house during the strawberry season." He would go on to contrast the heightened activities but, he believes, diminished efficiency of present-day clergy.

From Hedon he went to York, first to be house-master at St Peter's School, then to be Vicar of St Martin's, Coney Street. The schoolmaster episode was his one failure. He had insufficient patience, at least at that period of his life, with the average boy. As a York Vicar he became a man of affairs, especially in regard to educational administration. There and at Dewsbury, in the West Riding, he was Chairman of the School Board, a Governor of several Secondary Schools, a founder of others, and a prime mover in the investigations that resulted in the Education Act of 1902. At Melbourne his interest in education had full scope, and he will long be remembered in Australia as a founder and benefactor of Church Schools. Coming on both sides of a long line of 'statesmen' (small Cumberland and Westmorland farmers owning their own land), he had a supreme sense of value of the family, that each member should do his best to hand on the lamp. But he was large-minded enough to be almost equally keen on the education of other men's sons.

In 1902, when he was Vicar of Huddersfield, two Australian laymen were travelling through England on the look-out for a suitable man to recommend to their diocese as Bishop of Melbourne. Their choice fell on Henry Lowther Clarke. His consecration in St Paul's cathedral was one of the last public acts of Archbishop Temple.

The choice of the Committee was generally approved. The see had been administered for more than ten years by that great Bishop, James Moorhouse, afterwards of Manchester, who assisted in the consecration of Canon Clarke, and it was traditionally associated with a vigorous Broad Churchmanship, inclining to the Evangelical position, with which the new Bishop was definitely in sympathy. He was but 52 years old, and he possessed a great deal of experience of pastoral work in large industrial centres. In Australia Dr Clarke showed, as was indeed expected, remarkable administrative ability and energy, especially in promoting popular education, and he also made a reputation as a preacher of exceptional gifts. Not long after his arrival the five dioceses in the State of Victoria were constituted an ecclesiastical province, and in 1905 the Bishop of Melbourne, as Metropolitan, received the title of Archbishop. He took an active interest in the training of clergy, and was president of the Melbourne College of Divinity from 1911 to 1916, and a Fellow of the Australian College of Theology during his whole period in Australia. In 1904 he was appointed one of the six episcopal canons of the collegiate church of St George the Martyr at Jerusalem, his stall being entitled Pisgah, and at his death he was the senior canon.

The Lambeth Conference of 1920 was the culmination of his official career. He took a prominent part on the Committee which dealt with Reunion, but saw the difficulties more plainly than most of the Bishops, thanks to his experience in Australia of negotiations between Anglicans and Presbyterians.

After the Conference, on his seventieth birthday, the Archbishop resigned his see. Having been responsible for a measure which practically compelled the clergy to retire at that age, he felt that no other course was possible. He bought the house at Lymington, Hampshire, in which Coventry Patmore had lived, and settled down to enjoy his newly-found leisure. After fifty years' cessation from classical studies he began Latin and Greek again, soaking himself in Virgil and Horace, and making a translation of the whole of Homer with his own hand. (An attempt to read Plato was unsuccessful.) This was partly for recreation, but partly also with a view to forming a literary style, in which respect he felt himself to be deficient. His *History of Sedbergh School* (1925) shows that Homer had taught him how to tell a story, and *Death and the Hereafter* (1926) is a model of a simple exposition of a great theme. Besides these books he wrote after his retirement a massive volume on *Constitutional Church Government in the Anglican Communion* (1925), and many pamphlets and articles on a variety of subjects, including the antiquities of Hampshire. So long as his health lasted he preached constantly both in the neighbourhood and at a distance. And he played his part as a wise and moderating counselor in current Church movements, never seeking to overstep the limits necessarily imposed upon a retired bishop.

When Henry Lowther Clarke died in 1926, he left behind a world recovering from the most disastrous war that had ever been known. A war that had resulted in the death of more soldiers and sailors than any previous war, but not just fighting men; the atrocities in Belgium and France had touched the non-combatant women, old men, children and babies. The demand for men was such that their places in industry had been filled by their wives; workplaces that young women did not want to vacate. Joan Clarke and her sister Silvia would enter adolescence with a very different outlook on life than had their mother and aunts.

Education was the route by which the girls of the 1920s and 1930s would seek to escape the stereotypical roles of the previous generation. With her natural ability in mathematics Joan could expect to advance as far as she was able, rather than permitted. Of course, she was the product of an academic family, and a family that could afford to send her to a private school where her naturel abilities were free to develop. Most children, however talented, came from families which were in no position to let their sons, let alone their daughters, remain at school beyond the school leaving age, which in the 1920s was fourteen.

The 'war to end all wars' was over, but the 'land fit for heroes' had not yet been delivered. Problems, particularly in the coal industry led to discontent among the working population. The export market had been largely lost, and coal prices had been cut to the extent that the mine owners were steadily reducing miner's wages. Other industries were brought into the conflict; a General Strike was called but only lasted a few days. The miners held out for some weeks after the rest returned to work, but they eventually gave in and returned to the pits. The discontent was not limited to England and its allies.

In the defeated Germany, discontent with the terms of the Treaty of Versailles and with the government of the Weimar Republic, gave way to civil unrest, much more violent than in Britain. There was a call for re-armament and there was every indication that the next war, should there be one, would be more mechanised and more technological. Any future conflict would be even more mechanised, and even more driven by technology, than had been the previous one. Instant communication over long distances would be the key to any future war at sea; communication would need to be wireless and, with wireless communication, security would be of the greatest importance.

In Berlin, Dr Arthur Scherbius set up Chiffriermaschinen Aktiengesellschaft (Cipher Machines Corporation) to manufacture his *Enigma* machine which he hoped to sell to commercial companies, banks etc. *Enigma* allowed an operator to type in a message, then scramble it by means of three, four or five notched wheels, or rotors, which displayed different letters of the alphabet. The receiver needed to know the exact settings of these rotors in order to reconstitute the coded text. In 1926 his *Enigma* machine was adopted by the German Navy, with a few modifications, and went into service.

AUTHOR'S NOTE: Dr Arthur Scherbius first formed a company named Scherbius & Ritter that applied for a patent for a cipher machine based on rotating wired wheels, he also purchased the rights to another rotor machine from Hugo Koch, to be initially pitched at the commercial market. However, early attempts to find a market were frustrated because no one showed interest or even noticed his invention.

Trademark plate of Chiffriermaschinen Aktiengesellschaft, used on the commercial version of Enigma.
(acknowledgement https://de.wikiversity.org)

During the first war the breaking of coded messages had been the responsibility of the Admiralty's 'Room 40' and had been the route to frustrating German attempts to surprise the British fleet at the battles of Dogger Bank and of Jutland. The breaking of codes would become the province of mathematicians; and for which mathematicians of the highest calibre would be required. In 1925 Alan Turing was at Hazelhurst

Preparatory School in Frant; Joan Clarke was at elementary school in Dulwich. Both had a facility for mathematics; Turing had vision, while Joan had the determination to solve the problem; Turing to find a solution; Joan to see it through to a result.

The contribution that Joan Clarke was able to make to Britain's future was, in no small part, due to the influence of her grandfather. His enthusiasm for education, especially the education of girls, helped create an atmosphere in which his granddaughter could thrive and reach her full potential. Henry's enthusiasm for promoting education for girls can be seen by his purchasing of two schools on behalf of Diocese of Melbourne, merging them and thus founding Lowther Hall Anglican Grammar School for Girls.

> *AUTHOR'S NOTE: Lowther Hall still exists as a grammar school, providing education for girls. The school is based on the 'house' system, all named after former bishops and archbishops, including Clark House named in honour of Henry. With eight hundred girls the school still ranks as one of Melbourne's leading girls' schools.*

CHAPTER 4

GROWING UP IN THE SHADOWS

Joan Clarke's childhood was one lived in the shadow of the rise of fascism in Germany and Italy. In September 1921, when Joan was only four years old, the eyes of the world were watching the growing discontent within Germany, and the rising tide which would eventually lead to National Socialism, to the popularity of Adolf Hitler, and to a second world war breaking out during the first half of the twentieth century. An intelligent girl, she would become more and more aware of the political situation in Europe as she went through elementary and then high (grammar) school, and then to university. It would be difficult to imagine that any young person could go through the 1920s and the 1930s without it colouring their lives to some extent.

In September of 1921, while her grandfather and aunt were settling into their new home in Lymington and the south of England was beginning to obtain some relief from the very hot summer and the very long drought, the first indication was given of what would eventually prove to be the defining activity of Joan Clarke's life. Adolf Hitler's control of National Socialist German Workers' Party was gaining strength and his meetings were becoming less and less content to allow dissenting views to be voiced, and his meeting hall protection detachment became more and more effective in suppressing opposition to him. By November, after a particularly bloody confrontation at the Munich Hofbräuhaus, the group were renamed as *Sturmabteilung* or, more informally, as brownshirts.

> AUTHOR'S NOTE: The term Sturmabteilung predates the founding of the Nazi Party in 1919. Originally it was applied to the specialised assault troops of Imperial Germany during the First World War. Instead of large mass assaults, the Sturmabteilung were organised into multiple small groups. Hitler organised squads of ex-soldiers and beer hall brawlers into the Sturmabteilung to protect gatherings of the Nazi Party from disruption by the Social Democrats and Communists, and to disrupt the meetings of the other political parties.

Elsewhere, on the European mainland, Italy's move towards Fascism was begun when Benito Mussolini, following his 'March on Rome', became prime minister, taking the place of Luigi Facta who had been refused permission to declare martial law by King Victor Emmanuel III. Before the end of 1922 his *black-shirts* had taken over the role of a political police force, effectively achieving a coup without conflict. Mussolini formed a right-wing coalition government; Fascists, nationalists, liberals, and two clerics from the 'Popular Party'.

In Bavaria, encouraged by the *black-shirt's* March on Rome, Adolf Hitler with his *brownshirts* planned a march on Munich as a first step in his planned overthrow of the Weimar Republic government. An armed confrontation with State Police resulted in four police and sixteen Nazi deaths. The insurgents, including Hitler and an injured Göring, fled. Two days later Hitler was arrested and brought to trial, he and Rudolf Hess, another of his supporters, each receiving a five-year prison sentence.

Adolf Hitler used 1924, while he served his prison sentence in the old fortress at Landsberg, to write *Mein Kampf* (My Struggle) in which he spoke of his early days in the Nazi Party, and his future plans for Germany. He claimed that Germany must defeat its old enemy France and secure Germany's western border. He bitterly recalled the end of the First World War, saying the German Army had been denied victory on the battlefield by political treachery at home. Despite a five-year prison sentence, pressure from the Nazi party secured his release five days before Christmas of that year.

In 1927, Joan's eldest brother Basil was in his first year at St John's College, Durham after attending St John's School in Leatherhead, Surrey, before that at The Knowl School in Woburn Sands, and before that at a small local private school. St John's College had been founded as a Church of England theological college but, by the time that Basil attended, had became a full constituent college of the university; here he was following in the footsteps of his father and grandfather in studying theology with the intention of a clerical life in the Church. He went from Durham to theological college at Cuddesdon College, and was to be ordained in 1932 at the age of twenty-four.

Next eldest, Martin, was still at The Knowl School in Woburn Sands, which Martin described as very much a 'Cambridge' prep school, and Haileybury School in

Hertfordshire. He also mentioned that, having spent some time immediately previous to his going to Knowl staying with his uncle Francis and aunt Eva in the Bedfordshire village of Turvey, where he had been unable to quote the present indicative of the French verb *avoir*, resulting in him being placed in the lowest form. He persevered and did well at the school, eventually gaining a place at King's College, Cambridge in 1930 to begin his studies in the Classics.

Joan's sister, Silvia, had attended the kindergarten at Dulwich High School for Girls and then through the senior forms of that same school. Silvia did not follow the academic path of her older brothers but, on leaving school, began working as a secretary for the BBC in Portland Place.

> *AUTHOR'S NOTE: The British Broadcasting Corporation came into existence on 1 January 1927, having moved from being a private company to being a virtual arm of government, although claimed independence from political pressures. The reality was, however, slightly different, the BBC imposing a level of political censorship in conjunction with the Foreign Office, which maintained that the public should not be aware of their role in the censorship.*

Joan, the youngest member of the Clarke household was, as had been her sister, schooled at the kindergarten of Dulwich High School for Girls. Among previous pupils had been her brother Martin, at one point being the only boy among an entire school of girls. He had been removed from Mayfield School "one of those (doubtless ephemeral) small private schools which flourished in my youth" [7]. The Elementary Education Act of 1870 had required the establishment of elementary schools where existing provision was inadequate, and to be financed out of local rates. An appointed local School Board was charged with the management of the scheme on behalf of the government, the members of which often included the local clergy. However, many middle class families chose to support the small private schools or the kindergarten departments of a reputable prep school.

Joan eventually began her senior schooling at Dulwich High School for Girls on Thurlow Park Road. Here she was to develop, under the guidance of Miss Williams, her headmistress, a growing interest in and facility for mathematics. The school opened in the late nineteenth century as part of the Girls' Public Day School Trust, set up in response to a government enquiry into the shortage of education for women in England and pressure from the newly formed Women's Education Union, was one of a rash of similar schools opened across the country.

> *AUTHOR'S NOTE: The Girls' Public Day School Trust does still exist, although many of the schools that existed between the wars have since been closed or passed into other hands. Some of the remaining schools have now become co-educational.*

Joan's mother, Dorothy, in her garden at 193 Rosendale Road, Dulwich
(courtesy of John Clarke, Joan's nephew)

During the following few years developments in central Europe were at the forefront of people's concerns; that included Joan and her family, the general assumption being that Hitler was anti-religious to the extent that, given the sympathies held by many industrialists and members of the British upper class, the Established Church was fearful of the possible consequences. Such fears were reinforced by Hitler's appointment as Chancellor of Germany and, within three months, his proclamation of the Third Reich and the passing of the Enabling Act that made Adolf Hitler dictator of Germany.

The Clarke family was able to learn something of the German threat through Martin Clarke's travels in Europe during the early 1930s, visiting Greece, Italy, Austria and Germany. On visiting Germany for the first time he describes his landlady as *gebildet* (educated) and her niece as plump and agreeable with a slight hankering after Nazism. During his second trip to Germany he stayed with Professor Willich in Munich, as a paying guest. While politics were not a feature of their conversation, Martin wrote that it was well known that the Willich family did not think much of the Führer.

> Frauline Willich (the professor's sister) called upon the deity and gloomily inveighed, against politics in general whenever a new election came on, while the professor cheerfully dismissed Hitler and his followers as fools. Though Hitler addressed monster meetings and street clashes were reported. In English papers, Munich seemed quite calm. The papers were uninformative; we did not of course have the *Völkischen Beobachter*, whose shrill headlines denouncing Marxist corruption could be seen at the street corners but the respectable *Münchner Neueste Nachrichten*, which told one very much less about what was going on than the Berlin correspondent of *The Times*, which I often read in the library of the University. One evening as I came home I saw the announcement that Hitler had become Chancellor. The Willichs were plunged in gloom.

> But for the moment things were not serious, and there was a touch of comedy even about Hitler's accession to power. It had been a cold winter, with the snow frozen firmly on the streets; then a sudden thaw, and it was almost impossible to walk on the slippery pavements. The Nazis tried to parade about the streets singing their songs of triumph, but marching was quite impossible on that day, and they slithered about in helpless djsorder[8].

Dulwich High School for Girls also underwent significant changes during 1935-36, Joan's last year at Thurlow Park Road, as Miss Williams retired as headmistress and Miss N M Horobin took her place. The school prize-giving day was covered in more detail than usual by The Norwood News, carrying an address to the school by it's new headmistress, giving a clear indication of the more modern view of the future role of women in society than had, hitherto, been accepted.

"I want to insist on the old standards of courtesy, respect and reverence. As a nation, let us cling to them and make every effort to get away from the fatally easy destructive criticism to which we are prone, and to inspire in those for whom we are responsible the ability to appreciate. To all that is best in our national institutions, to our Christian religion, to all that is true, pure and lovely and of good report, to all these things let us cling with courage and a belief in our own ideals."

Miss Horobin said they were preparing girls to meet life as they found it, and as girls had gone out from that school in past years successfully prepared, they were anxious to do the same for the present girls, and if that were to be so, they must keep pace with the changing world, whilst holding fast to principles which never changed. They must aim at individual development within the responsibilities they owed to the social community in which they lived. Ever widening opportunities lay before their girls and those in school had a great responsibility. While at school they must learn to take the rough with the smooth.

Miss Horobin went on to say that she would like girls to remain at least one year in the sixth form. It was not only that in that form the scholarly side of life began to make it's appeal, but that in the sixth form the true value of learning became more apparent, critical faculties developed and the whole life of school was seen from a different angle. It was in the sixth form that girls learned true self-discipline and the power to accept responsibility, both such necessary factors in life to-day. In other parts of the school they hoped also to encourage independent thought and the right use of leisure. If with the increasing use of machinery they were to have more leisure, then let them use their privileges well.

At the school they were to try the experiment of less set work to be done out of school hours, in order that the girls might develop hobbies and approach lessons with contributions of knowledge achieved by their own free efforts. Miss Horobin mentioned that she wanted to build an open-air classroom, where the kindergarten could do most of their work in the summer term, and other forms, when possible, could benefit by fresh air.

Joan Lowther Clarke was named as the recipient of one of the 'special' prizes, and it seems that as she left school she began to incorporate her given name 'Lowther' as part of her surname; although she never hyphenated it as Lowther-Clarke, reinstating Lowther as one of her 'given' names in later years. Miss Williams had been Joan's headmistress during her entire time at the High School, and she had benefited from Miss Williams' improving standard of tuition and resultant success in examination results.

Joan, aged nineteen, during her final year at school.
(courtesy of John Clarke, Joan's nephew)

The start of Michaelmas Term at Newnham College, Cambridge saw Joan Clarke living in college rooms and ready to begin her studies. Head of the Newnham College was Joan Pernel Strachey, a sixty-year old ex-student at Newnham, and closely connected with the Bloomsbury Group and Virginia Woolf; she had a background in the suffragist movement and was a leading campaigner to get real degrees for women at Girton and Newnham colleges. A campaign that was unsuccessful, one that would take until 1947 until finally won.

Joan's older brother Martin was already in Cambridge and, as was only natural, he took an interest in her assimilation into the ways of the university. There was a social life in Cambridge that reflected the middle-class standing of the majority of students; teashops and picnics being most popular for mixed sex groups, the public bars being more of a male preserve. Ladies, as against 'women' did not tend to frequent pubs and the Rev. William Kemp Lowther Clarke would have been somewhat displeased if Martin had introduced Joan into that world.

In December of 1936 Edward VIII, having become king on the death of his father earlier that year, abdicated in order to marry Wallis Simpson, an American divorcee. Joan, in common with most young women, most young people even, in the country would be on the side of 'romance'. Their marriage, the following June in the Château de Candé, one month after Wallis Simpson's divorce, was a very low key event as far as the British were concerned. Joan certainly had more to occupy her mind at Newnham College, than girlish romanticism.

King's College, was one of the most prestigious of the Cambridge colleges, located in the centre of the city in King's Parade, with gardens sweeping down to the river, where punts were available for picnic groups or for more intimate twosomes along the Cam and into secluded farmland moorings. Martin had 'rooms' in King's College, ideally situated; Newnham College was some distance away from the centre and so Joan and her fellow female students gravitated towards the centre of Cambridge. The void between 'town' and 'gown' was wide, even wider for female students, and the imbalance in numbers between the sexes made the walk or bicycle ride into the centre of Cambridge, well worth it.

Quite close to Martin Clarke's rooms, in King's College, were those of twenty-three year old Alan Mathison Turing, studying mathematics and elected as a Fellow of the college earlier that year. Although their fields of study were very different, the two men knew each other reasonably well and Martin introduced Turing to his sister, aware of their mutual interest in mathematics.

With the threat of war increasing, life in England was changing at an alarming pace. In June the Women's Voluntary Service was founded to assist the Civil Defence Service, in July gas masks were issued to the civilian population, and in September the Munich Agreement was signed with Neville Chamberlain returning from Germany, waving the paper and giving his 'Peace in our time' speech. Before the end of the year the first Jewish children arrived from Germany, Austria, Czechoslovakia and Poland as part of the *Kindertransport* rescue as a response to the *Kristallnacht* or the 'night of broken glass'. The British establishment was beginning to take the threat of war more and more seriously.

> *AUTHOR'S NOTE: A telegram informed all police units in Germany that action would be taken on the night of 9th November (Kristallnach) against Jews, synagogues and businesses across the country. Their instructions were that these actions should not be interfered with but, rather, the police should arrest the victims. Fire fighters were specifically instructed that the buildings should be left to burn, and to only intervene should adjacent Aryan properties be threatened.*

In the summer of 1938 Alan Turing, the man destined to have a considerable influence on Joan's life, had returned to England from his visit to America. With the looming threat of war with Germany, Turing was invited to attend a course on cryptology at the Government Code and Cipher School (GC&CS), where he indicated his willingness to contribute to their work if war were to be declared. After the summer course at GC&CS he returned to King's College for the start of the Michaelmas term. On returning to live in 'rooms' at the college Turing found himself, once again, living just down the landing to his old acquaintance Martin Clarke.

On 29th September 1939, the Government carried out a survey in order to create an accurate register of everyone in the country, men, women and children, whatever their nationality. National Registration was intended to facilitate food rationing, so households were instructed to leave a forwarding address if they moved before ration books were sent out, due some weeks later. William and Dorothy Clarke, Joan's parents, were still living at 193 Rosendale Road and Joan was staying with them for the holidays. Described as a University Student, she was also identified as being a member of the Cambridge Red Cross detachment working as a nursing auxiliary. Joan's brother Martin, being a Fellow was resident at King's; her brother Basil, now a minister of religion, was married and living in Winchester Road, Oxford at his first parish. Joan's sister Silvia was living with three other BBC secretaries in Seaford Court, Great Portland Street.

> *AUTHOR'S NOTE: Anticipated civilian injuries from air raids prompted the formation of The Civil Nursing Reserve, which meant recruiting young women to become voluntary nursing auxiliaries. The volunteers were given training and a blue uniform with white apron bib and 'Halifax' cap. Voluntary work of this type was particularly suited to university students who were able to fit their duties in with their studies.*

In September Germany invaded Poland and, in response, the United Kingdom, France, New Zealand and Australia declared war, quickly followed by South Africa and Canada in quick succession. U-Boats were already attacking British ships, the SS *Athenia* and HMS *Royal Oak* being sunk but the German *Admiral Graf Spee* was scuttled by its crew off Montevideo harbour after a running battle with HMS *Ajax*, *Exeter* and *Achilles*. In Britain compulsory military service was announced; the war had begun and Alan Turing was called upon to fulfill his obligation to GC&CS and instructed to present himself at Bletchley Park, north of London.

What Turing found at Bletchley Park was a country house estate, comprising a mansion, an ornamental lake and various outbuildings such as a cottage, stables and one or two wooden huts. The estate had been purchased in May 1938 by Admiral Hugh Sinclair who was Director of GC&CS, in anticipation of the start of war. There were already more than one hundred and fifty people working at Station-X, as Bletchley Park was more properly called, most of whom were billeted in Bletchley and surrounding villages; some in pubs, some in hotels, some in private homes. The term 'Captain Ridley's Shooting Party' has been used to identify the early days of Bletchley Park, but in reality the term belies the gravity and intensity of the task facing them.

The Mansion at Bletchley Park

(author's photograph)

Bletchley Park was not all about *Enigma*; it was about gathering, understanding and disseminating intelligence information intercepted by GC&CS through its listening posts, or Y-stations, distributed around the coast of Britain and further abroad. Turing, a mathematician found himself working with classics scholars, chess players, language professors; some civilian, some military. Recruitment of suitable personnel was a priority, and those staff members who had been previously employed in a teaching capacity at Oxford or Cambridge were pressed to identify suitable candidates.

Late in 1939, Joan received a letter from Gordon Welchman, who had supervised her in geometry, and was now at GC&CS in its new location at Bletchley Park. Although the address for reply was given as a room at the Foreign Office in London as the Buckinghamshire address was top secret, even its existence was unknown outside of a select few. In the letter Welchman offered her 'interesting' work with the government, unspecified but in a field to which mathematicians were particularly adept. Her reply was enthusiastic but she preferred to continue at Cambridge until the following summer, to complete Part III of the Mathematical Tripos, after which she would happily join Welchman.

In May 1940, while Joan was spending her last few days at Cambridge, significant changes were happening in the prosecution of the war. Neville Chamberlain had resigned as Prime Minister, his position being taken by Winston Churchill leading a coalition war government. One of the first crises for the new War Cabinet to face was the evacuation of the British Expeditionary Force from the beaches of Dunkirk, completed by 4th June. A week later, Italy declared war on France and Britain, and a week after that Joan Elisabeth Lowther Clarke arrived at Bletchley railway station ready to begin working on her own contribution to the war effort.

CHAPTER 5

HMS GLEANER AND U-33

In the early hours of 12th February 1940, the minesweeper HMS *Gleaner* (J83), captained by Lt-Commander Hugh Percival Price, was patrolling the outer reaches of the Firth of Clyde. She was a Halcyon-class minesweeper, with a crew of eighty, and armed with two 4-inch anti-aircraft guns and eight .303 machineguns. In addition to her regular armament she carried, and could deploy, up to forty depth charges; this was how she was configured when sailing as part of the 3rd Anti-Submarine Striking Force.

At 2:50am the hydrophone operator on board HMS *Gleaner* heard what sounded like a diesel engine and Lt-Commander Price gave the order to steer towards the target, about two miles off the port bow. As the distance between HMS *Gleaner* and the target narrowed, *Gleaner's* searchlights were turned on in time for the lookouts to see the small white spray of a submarine's periscope cutting through the water and disappearing from sight beneath the waves. With *Gleaner's* sonar equipment (ASDIC) locked on she dropped her first pattern of four depth charges just before 4:00am.

AUTHOR'S NOTE: ASDIC (Anti Submarine Division + supersonIC) was a carefully kept secret of the Royal Navy and was not shared with America until September 1940. There were practical limitations on its use in conjunction with the deployment of depth charges as that involved passing the submarine directly overhead, which gave the U-Boat an opportunity to take evasive action, and left the surface vessel blind for a short time. As the war continued the Americans began to use their own term SONAR.

The quarry was the German submarine *U-33*, under the command of Kapitanleutnant Hans von Dresky and a crew of forty-two. The submarine had left Heligoland on the 7th, passed between Orkney and Shetland and into the channel that lies between northern Ireland and Scotland. On the morning of 11th February, as dawn broke *U-33* lay on the bottom in two hundred feet of water waiting for nightfall, when it could surface and sow the mines that were intended for the entrance to the Firth of Clyde. At 2:00am on the 12th February the submarine surfaced and headed towards the Clyde.

Hugh Price's orders were to patrol the twenty-five fathom contour line outside the Firth of Clyde, which meant a triangular course, taking *Gleaner* close to the island of Ailsa Craig which lay to the south of the Isle of Arran, some twelve miles distant. HMS *Gleaner* was not alone in the Firth of Clyde that night; *U-33* had already silently passed a British cruiser at anchor, and was running as quietly as possible without jeopardising her mission.

U-33 being first spotted on the surface, and while crash-diving, took some damage from HMS *Gleaner's* depth charges and settled on the sea floor. At 4:40am the submarine suffered a further damaging attack and prepared to surface, intending to make way on the surface, strewing mines astern to impede pursuit. As a precaution, Dresky ordered the second watch officer Lt Johannes Becker to make preparations to destroy the submarine's *Enigma* machine and its rotors, three in the machine and a further five in the wooden box. Becker distributed the eight rotors between various crewmembers with instructions to drop the rotors into the water once they left the submarine.

U-33 lifted a little off the bottom and began to move slowly forward, but with the tide moving at six knots, steering was impossible and it soon became obvious that the original idea of a surface escape was not practical. The submarine began to take in water; there had been a small leak discovered in the port torpedo tube before reaching Heligoland, but had been sealed with a wood and rubber bung. With his store of compressed air almost exhausted, Dresky had little alternative but to use the air in the torpedo tubes and ordered as rapid a rise to the surface as possible.

At 5:22am the submarine surfaced and took five rounds from the British 4-inch gun. The order to abandon ship was given, the crew took to the water and by 5:30am the submarine had been scuttled; First Engineer Friedrich Schilling gave his account later:

> It was freezing cold, a pitch black night, very stormy with a rolling sea.
> I realized that our chances of rescue were not good. We could see lights
> glowing in the distance but no evidence of rescue vessels approaching.
> Initially, I found myself in a large group of boatmates. From time to
> time someone would plaintively ask: "Will they come and rescue us?"

to which I replied: "They will come alright, lad. Hold on. Keep swimming. Give it everything you've got." Some shadows appeared.

"I did not want to go under so I kept on swimming, concentrating on those shadows ahead. I did not feel the cold and never gave up hope but our group became smaller and smaller. At the end all that remained were Johne, Weber, Keller and some others who swam right behind us.

All of a sudden a searchlight stabbed out, just a short distance away. "We've made it," I shouted. "Come on." I saw a high hull and grabbed at a rope hanging from the side. Next to me I saw Obergefreiter Weber hanging on to another rope. I don't know what happened next and I must have fallen unconscious[9].

Two British trawlers, *Floradora* and *Bohemian Girl*, made for the location and picked up some survivors, as did the destroyer HMS *Kingston*. In all, twenty-five Germans died, mainly due to exhaustion and hypothermia, including the Commanding Officer Hans-Wilhelm von Dresky; seventeen survivors were handed over to the authorities and later transferred, first for interrogation and then to a Prisoner of War camp; the dead were buried in Greenock cemetery.

Five of the *Enigma* rotors were released into the sea, but three were forgotten and found their way into the hands of the Royal Navy to be passed on, eventually finding their way to Bletchley Park and into the hands of Alan Turing and his small team of cryptanalysts. Of the three rotors captured, two, numbers VI and VII, were ones for which the wiring was previously unknown. The wiring for the first five rotors had been established by Polish cryptanalysts before the war; only the wiring of the eighth rotor now eluded Bletchley Park.

The eight rotors were the primary encryption process at the root of the *Enigma* machine. Each rotor had twenty-six electrical contacts on either side of the wheel, each input contact was connected, or hardwired, to a contact on the output side according to a pre-determined pattern. On a typewriter style keyboard, each key could be connected to a contact on the input side of the rotor, sending an electrical charge through the rotor when that key was depressed. The charge would travel through the rotor's hardwiring to a contact on the output side of the rotor, which was then connected to the corresponding light on the display. Each input key corresponded to a letter of the alphabet, and each output display light displayed a letter of the alphabet. Thus depressing the letter **C** might display the letter **Y**; depressing the letter **Q** might display the letter **F** and so on.

A further level of security was achieved by mounting three rotors, side by side, on a spindle with the output contact from the first rotor directly connected to the input contact of the second rotor, and the output contact from the second rotor being directly connected to the input contact of the third rotor; the output contact of the third rotor being connected to a light on the display. Thus the depression of the **C** key might result in C to Y: Y to H: H to S resulting in the **S** being displayed. Each *Enigma* machine was supplied with a set of rotors, in most cases a set of five, but for German naval codes a set of eight, each of which was differently hardwired.

In use, the *Enigma* operator needed to select which rotors, identified as I to VIII, would be used on any specific day, and in which order they should be positioned on the spindle: left, centre or right. Depending upon the rotors chosen and their sequence on the spindle, even knowing the hardwiring of each rotor presented a significant hurdle to decryption. A further complication was achieved by the operator being able to set the starting position of each rotor; thus if the left rotor were positioned such that the **C** key pointed to input contact Q instead of C then the output to the centre rotor would be quite different and so on across the three rotors to the output display.

The final obstacle to decryption lay in *Enigma's* ability to constantly change during use. Each rotor was built with a toothed gear wheel incorporated; each time that a key was depressed the right hand wheel turned one position so that even if the same key was depressed multiple times a different character would be illuminated each time. When the right-hand rotor had completed a full revolution then the middle rotor would turn one position and so on to the left-hand rotor; each cycle not repeating for 26 x 26 x 26 (17,576) key depressions.

The same *Enigma* machine could be used for both encryption and decryption of messages. This was achieved by use of a plugboard (*Steckerbrett*) that paired letters so that if, for example, C converted to Y then Y would convert to C, if H converted to S then S would convert to H, etc. The initial setting of this plugboard constituted a further variable; the generally accepted possible ways of setting up Enigma became a formidable 100,391,791,500, or more than one hundred trillion.

The initial setting of the *Enigma* machine for each period, day or week, was specified in terms of which rotors to use and in which order, their starting positions and the plugboard pairings. The initial settings for each day or week were contained in codebooks for the operator to use and constituted the secret papers that the ship's officers were charged with destroying when their vessel was in danger of being captured.

The Cottage at Bletchley Park

(author's photograph)

Armed with knowledge of how the internal hardwiring of each rotor type was configured allowed Turing and the Seniors in Bletchley mansion's stable yard, known as 'The Cottage', to employ mechanical means to assist with determining the *Enigma* settings for a given message and therefore, hopefully, all the messages for that day or group of days. An attempt to empirically deduce the codebook settings from very little information, more often than not a guess as to what a specific message might contain, perhaps a time or date, perhaps a simple "Guten Tag" or "Auf Wiedersehen" perhaps "Heil Hitler" or "Vaterland".

> Useful information came from prisoners of war. The revelation by a captured enemy Funkmaat (radio petty officer) called Meyer in November 1939 that the German Navy always spelled out numerals in full meant that EINS (one) became the commonest tetragram in German Naval traffic – at least one EINS featured in 90 per cent of messages. An EINS catalogue could be made by enciphering EINS at all the 16,900 positions of the machine on the keys of the days in question, and then comparing it with other messages of the day for repeats[10].

The machine employed to assist the codebreakers was the *Bombe* or *Bomba Kryptologiczna*, an electro-mechanical device originally invented by Polish Cipher Bureau cryptologists. The three rotors of the *Enigma* were replicated within the *Bombe* as a single set, but repeated in a bank of thirty-six sets all linked together. Each of the eight types of rotor, colour coded, were available to make up the thirty-six sets such that when the *Bombe* was set in motion it could explore multiple possible *Enigma* settings.

When Poland was invaded by the Germans in September 1939 the Polish cryptanalysts escaped Warsaw by way of Romania to finally reach the Château de Vignolles at Gretz-Armainvilliers in France to join the French cryptanalysts. Jerzy Różycki, Henryk Zygalski and Marian Rejewski, having had all their equipment and paperwork confiscated in Romania, continued work with Gustave Bertrand, chief of French radio intelligence at PC Bruno, the French equivalent of Bletchley Park.

The original Polish design was somewhat limited in scope and complexity, but did form the basis of the *Bombe* designed by Alan Turing and built at British Tabulating Machine Company in Letchworth; named *Victory* it was installed in Hut 1 at Bletchley Park in March 1940 in time to include the settings for rotors VI and VII, recovered from *U-33* on the 12th of the previous month. Although no messages were being decrypted Bletchley Park was gaining insights into the process and learning how to recognise and exploit the weaknesses in *Enigma* and the German procedures for employing it.

AUTHOR'S NOTE: The British Tabulating Machine Company (BTM) was licenced to market Hollerith punched card equipment from the American owned Tabulating Machine Company (TMC later IBM). By the outbreak of war BTM had developed an engineering capability of its own and was manufacturing under its own name.

Much of the credit for understanding the original *Enigma* machine must go to Marian Rejewski who had attended Poznań University and then began working for the Polish Cipher Bureau in Warsaw where he was joined by Jerzy Różycki and Henryk Zygalski. The three Polish cryptanalysts managed to determine the internal wiring of the original five rotors, and the manner in which *Enigma* operated, by purely mathematical means without ever seeing the military machine. Rejewski had begun working part-time for the Poznań Branch of the Polish Cipher Bureau having first attended a cryptology course run by the university for the best German speaking mathematics students.

One weakness evident to the Bletchley Park codebreakers was *Enigma's* ability to perform both encryption and decryption using identical settings. The pairing of letters, such that if C converted to Y then Y would convert to C, or if H converted to S then S would convert to H, meant that no letter in plain text could ever be encrypted to itself. The more logical, if less efficient, method of using one machine to encrypt and another to decrypt, or to simply have an encrypt/decrypt switch on the machine, had shown the cryptanalysts at the Polish Cipher Bureau a basic weakness that they could exploit; a weakness that Bletchley Park went on to exploit still further.

The second weakness was obligated by the need to confirm the selection and order of the rotors to the recipient. This was achieved by sending a three character signal to identify the rotor selection and order, left to right. These three characters were transmitted as the first part of each message, but were repeated to form a six-character heading. This was thought to be safe, as although the plain text would show a repetition, the encrypted text would appear quite random. However, knowing how each rotor was hardwired and knowing the step mechanism of one rotor to another, allowed the Bletchley Park mathematicians to gain a little insight into the other possible settings.

There was more than one signal protocol, or system, employed across the German forces. The German Navy (*Kriegsmarine*) also employed a short signal book (*Kurzsignalheft*) and a weather short signal book (*Wetterkurzschlüssel*). The main home-waters communication protocol, for communication with the U-Boat wolf packs was named *Heimische Gewässer* in German, but within Bletchley Park was known as *Dolphin*.

In early 1940 the different *Enigma* systems were divided among the chief cryptanalysts who were allocated huts outside the Bletchley mansion. Welchman took over the army and air force *Enigma* systems, in Hut 6, joined by a number of new recruits. Dillwyn Knox took on the Italian Enigma and that used by the German SD, again with new recruits. These systems, which did not use plugboards, suited his psychological methods. And Alan [Turing] was allocated Hut 8 in which to head the work on the naval *Enigma* signals. Other huts housed sections translating and interpreting the output; thus Hut 3 dealt with the army and air force material issuing from Hut 6, while the naval signals, if and when they were produced, would be interpreted by Hut 4, which was headed by Frank Birch[20].

The team at Bletchley Park, headed by Alan Turing, was made up with three others who might, at first sight, have constituted a mismatched group. Gordon Welchman had studied mathematics at Trinity College, Cambridge and later was a Research Fellow at Sidney Sussex College where he had supervised Joan Clarke in Geometry while she was at the university. Dillwyn 'Dilly' Knox was, by contrast, a classics scholar at King's College but transferred to GS&CS as a cryptanalyst in time to be involved in the transfer of knowledge from the Polish codebreakers to their British counterparts. Frank Birch, again a product of King's College, was an historian and a pre-war film actor of some note.

Gordon Welchman, Joan's tutor at Cambridge

(internet image)

The method by which the codebreakers used *Bombe* to assist them was to capitalise on *Enigma's* weakness of never allowing a character in plain text to encrypt to that same character in enciphered text. The method was, therefore, to attempt to decipher an intercepted encrypted message and comparing the resultant 'plain text' to the original, character by character. If the same letter ever appeared in the corresponding position in both texts then it meant that the initial setting was 'false', i.e. not a valid *Enigma* setting, and could be discounted. Each running cycle of the *Bombe* could examine thirty-six possible settings, each cycle taking twenty minutes, three per hour, seventy-two per day; something of a surprise that any decryptions were accomplished, those that were coming weeks after the events which they may have augured.

Turing also exploited the pairing weakness of *Enigma* by incorporating modifications that made use of known, or likely, text at specific parts of the message, usually at the beginning or end. This meant that the *Bombe* could be set to search for these *cribs,* which made for fewer, more productive runs. Traffic analysis of intercepted German messages became a vital part of the information fed to the cryptanalysts by the linguistic experts, familiar not only with the language but with the military jargon and shorthand of the different services. The longer the *crib*, the greater its potential value, since being able to quickly discount an incorrectly guessed *Enigma* setting was valuable in itself.

Although the *Bombe* made a significant contribution to the mechanics of decryption, it was not the solution. Its contribution was simply to reduce the number of possibilities that the cryptanalysts had to consider. The breaking of the *Enigma* code was still down to the skill of the codebreakers; whether they employed mathematics or more prosaic means, the breaking of *Enigma* was simply down to the application of human intellect. This is what Welchman meant when he described the task as not being mathematics, but something that "mathematicians were good at".

March 1940 passed with Bletchley Park cryptanalysts making some progress in breaking *Enigma*, but not nearly fast enough to be of practical use. What Turing and his colleagues required to make progress was more insight into the relationship between plain text and encrypted text, and sight of operational codebooks used by the German Navy and, on the technical front, there needed to be a significant speed improvement in the way that the *Bombe* operated.

CHAPTER 6

HMS GRIFFIN AND VP2623/POLARIS

Florrie Foord went below the waves for a third time. His grip on the heaving line thrown from the whaler lost to his grasp for a second time; the first attempt to recover him from the icy waters off Narvik, where the April sea temperature averages only 6°C above freezing, had been equally frustrating. He had held on to the rope with a single hand, but the violent water had made him lose his grasp and the weight of the bag that he held in his other hand had forced him down into the sea.

Foord surfaced again, his left arm held below the surface, his right arm stretching skywards desperate for another attempt at rescue. This time a bowline was thrown, with a substantial loop secured by the eponymous knot, which he managed to get his head and right arm through, then transferring his trophy to his right hand, forced the other through the loop. The bag was taken from him as he was pulled alongside the whaler, willing hands pulled him from the water and into the 'prize' boat.

The naval action had begun just before 7am that morning when a British destroyer, HMS *Arrow* had been rammed by a trawler flying a Dutch flag, changed at the last moment to the Kriegsmarine flag of the German Navy. HMS *Arrow* was holed but the British destroyer HMS *Birmingham* fired four salvos to sink the German undercover mine layer. HMS *Arrow* with two other destroyers, *Griffin* and *Acheron*, went in search of more Dutch trawlers; at 10:15am they sighted another one, *Polares*, with the word 'Holland' written on her sides.

HMS *Griffin* approached the trawler and saw that she was armed with two torpedo tubes and a false canvas structure in the stern, confirming that she was not a simple fishing vessel, and so sent an armed boarding party in a whaler to board her. Before the boarding party could draw alongside, one of the trawler's crew threw two bags over the side, one sinking immediately, the other floating towards *Griffin*; grappling irons were deployed but the bag could not be recovered. This was the moment that Florrie Foord, a member of the prize crew that had been dispatched in the whaler, jumped into the sea to recover the barely floating second bag.

Polaris was actually the German patrol boat VP2623[11], originally the *Julius Pickenpack*, and found to be headed for Narvik carrying artillery pieces, magnetic mines, various explosives and a Browning machine gun. A skeleton crew sailed the captured vessel to the Orkneys, under the command of Alec Dennis, who had led the boarding party with German stokers working under guard and the Bavarian chef cooking huge meals of Danish bacon and eggs[21]. The British crew was triumphant over the capture and had already helped themselves to some small 'souvenirs'.

When *Griffin's* prize entered Scapa Flow she was flying the White Ensign over the Swastika, an event which was filmed by a Universal Film crew. When Lt. George Pennell from Naval Intelligence arrived in the Orkneys to take possession of the contents of the bag recovered from the sea, he discovered that it contained, among other papers, Enigma code books. Pennell's first action, on 4th May, was to seize the film and to put a security block on publicising the capture. For the capture of the secret documents to be considered a true intelligence coup it was important that their loss should be hidden from Germany.

> More might have been achieved if VP2623 had not been looted by her captors before she could be carefully searched; and the Admiralty at once issued instructions designed to prevent such disastrous carelessness in the future[12].

The 'Narvik Pinch' documents were sent to Bletchley Park where they were found to contain Enigma keys, some examples of plain and ciphered text, plugboard settings, and keys to the bigram or 'two letter' tables that the German Navy employed as a further security. The information, like that from U-33, found its way to Alan Turing and his team, now relocated to Hut 8.

By the time the 'Narvik Pinch' had been delivered to Naval Intelligence in London, examined and evaluated and finally found its way to Bletchley Park, there was a new member of the Hut 8 team in place. Joan Clarke had been recruited by Alan Turing, over Gordon Welchman's head, and had already found herself promoted to be one of the senior cryptanalysts. Clarke was much more suited to work with mathematician Turing, rather than with the more intuitive Welchman, and quickly began to make a real and significant contribution, following a quick introduction to the workings of *Enigma*.

With the aid of the 'Narvik Pinch' the team in Hut 8 managed to read some naval traffic from April but, although successful in its own right, not early enough to be of any real strategic value. Although the *Bombe* was proving its worth, time continued to be the critical factor in establishing its true value. Some of the successful decrypts were still down to solutions by pencil and paper, and sheer brainpower.

Alan Turing had come to the conclusion that the Germans enciphered the naval *Enigma* signals using a common starting position for the rotors (*Grundstellung*), and then applied bigram and trigram lookup tables contained within a *Kenngruppenbuch* book. The 'Narvik Pinch' had included plugboard connections and the *Grundstellung* for certain days, and a long stretch of paired plaintext and enciphered text for other days. The bigram tables themselves were not recovered, but Joan and her colleagues were able to partly reconstruct them and make the first attempt to employ *Banburismus*.

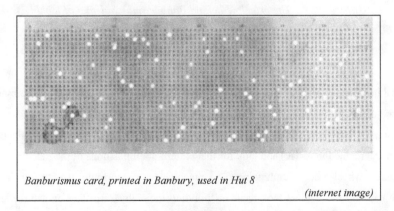

Banburismus card, printed in Banbury, used in Hut 8

(internet image)

Banburismus capitalised on the weakness of using a *Grundstellung* which was then the same for all messages on a particular day (or pair of days), which meant that it could happen that at some point in a message the rotor positions became the same as the starting position of the rotors for another message. This meant that there could be places within the encrypted texts of multiple messages where there was duplication, which would lead to an indication of the *Grundstellung*. The task was made easier by punching each character of text into the column of a card (top row=A, bottom row=Z) in the manner of a continuous stream. Each card was 10" high to accommodate the twenty-six character punch holes, and could be anything up to a few feet long to accommodate longer messages. The cards were printed in Banbury in Oxfordshire and became known as 'banburies' at Bletchley Park, and the procedure as *Banburismus*.

Banburismus did not identify *Grundstellung* settings directly, but provided a statistical probability of the correct setting of the right-hand rotor. *Banburismus* was used as a preliminary process to the employment of the *Bombe* or as an aid to calculating the *Grundstellung* settings by hand. Further processing could be used to test the middle rotor setting, although needing much longer messages, but the process was impractical to use on the left-rotor settings. Joan Clarke was the only female working on *Banburismus*, and was said to have been one of the best Banburists and was so enthusiastic and fascinated with the technique that she would sometimes be unwilling to hand over her workings at the end of her shift and would continue to see if a few more tests would produce a result[13].

> *AUTHOR'S NOTE: The principle behind Banburismus was that of looking for coincidence of characters greater than random expectation of 1:26 and that this allowed an attacker to test for congruity. The comparison of messages was made easier by punching the messages onto thin cards and then comparing one to the other, character by character.*

Hut 8 had a small special-purpose machine named *Baby*, which had been made by the same Letchworth company that manufactured the *Bombe*, the function of which was to continually encipher the four-letter German word EINS (expected to be contained in every intercepted message) and look for that pattern at all positions of the machine with the day's wheel-order and plugging. This machine ran for virtually twenty-four hours each day and the Seniors took turns in 'minding the Baby', working on a three shift system; Joan was very soon included in the rota and felt "quite important" as a consequence.

Very soon I worked a night shift, alone in Hut 8, and I felt quite important . . . Peter Twinn lent me his alarm clock so that I could relieve him at 2:am . . . The minder had to make regular checks, and set the Baby for a new start when a cycle was completed. By sorting and collating the encipherments of EINS with the message texts, the starting position could be obtained for a good proportion of the messages which had to be set individually at this stage because of the complexity of the naval indicating system. Using the *eins* catalogue and, at a later stage, 'twiddling' on messages for which part of the message was known, were enjoyable jobs which were shared by everyone in Hut 8. [14]

Joan's contribution to the work at Bletchley Park was soon rewarded, in the typically bureaucratic manner of government departments, by promotion to linguist grade, despite answering 'none' to a question about her knowledge of foreign languages, preferring not to mention school French and a smattering of German and Italian from reading mathematical books. The improved grade still did not qualify her to receive a monthly salary, like all female staff she was still paid weekly, and significantly less than male mathematicians who were not even regarded as Seniors.

Beyond Bletchley Park, the war continued. The evacuation of the British Expeditionary Force from Dunkirk had been completed before Joan had began work. Losses of men, equipment and ships were heavy and with approximately one in every seven members of the BEF being taken prisoner, very few of the population were unaffected. The heroism of the 'little ships' was of little consequence to the families of the forty thousand British soldiers taken off the beaches as prisoners of war to work in Germany.

July saw the beginning of 'The Battle of Britain' with intense bombing raids on London and other towns and cities. Rural areas did not escape the Luftwaffe's attentions, especially where the Germans were aware of industrial or intelligence activity taking place. Bletchley Park was on full alert, although it did not experience a direct hit until towards the end of 1940.

AUTHOR'S NOTE: In October 1940 a German aircraft strafed a railway train standing at Bletchley railway station and then attempted to bomb the station. They failed to hit the station, three bombs falling onto open ground, but one falling close to Hut 4 inside the Bletchley Park perimeter. Following the bombing, an anti-aircraft battery was sited between the railway station and Bletchley Park.

The Seniors in Hut 8 realised that the 'Narvik Pinch' had made an extraordinary contribution to the progress of their work and, using Turing as a conduit, made representations to the security services about actively seeking opportunities to secure further 'pinches', even to contrive methods by which pinches could be engineered.

Another pinch was needed if Dolphin was to be broken for any substantial period. Various plans were discussed. One, code-named Operation Ruthless, was masterminded by Lt. Cdr. Ian Fleming of Naval Intelligence, who later created the character James Bond . . . Operation Ruthless was not carried out[15].

The Operation Ruthless plan had been for a captured German bomber, crewed with German speakers, to follow on behind aircraft returning to Germany from a night bombing raid. Mid channel the aircraft would cut one engine and lose height with smoke pouring from the tail, send out a SOS distress signal and then ditch in the sea; the crew taking to a rubber dinghy and awaiting rescue by a German naval vessel. Once on board the rescue craft 'survivors' would then kill the German crew and hijack the vessel, thus obtaining the sought after *Enigma* documentation. The hijack crew waited for some time in Dover for a suitable bombing raid but aerial reconnaissance failed to find any suitable German rescue vessels, and the operation was called off.

Turing and Twinn came to me like undertakers cheated of a nice corpse two days ago, all in a stew about the cancellation of Operation Ruthless. The burden of their song was the importance of a pinch. Did the authorities realise that, since the Germans did the dirt on their machine on June 1st, there was very little hope, if any, of their deciphering current, or even approximately current, enigma for months and months and months - if ever? Contrariwise, if they got a pinch - even enough to give a clue to one day's material, they could be pretty sure, after an initial delay, of keeping going from day to day from then on; nearly up-to-date if not quite, because the level of traffic now is so much higher and because the machinery has been so much improved. The 'initial delay' would be in proportion to the pinch. If the whole bag of tricks was pinched, there'd be no delay at all. They asked me to add - what is self-evident - that they couldn't guarantee that at some future date, near or remote, the Germans mightn't muck their machine about again and necessitate another pinch. There are alternative operations possible. I put up one suggestion myself, and there are probably lots better, is there anything in the wind? I feel there ought to be[16].

Alan Turing wrote an account of *Enigma* theory for the purpose of introducing new cryptanalysts to the work at Bletchley Park, not just those in Hut 8, although Joan admitted that much of its contents were new to her. One chapter of 'Prof's Book' explained a method by which much more could have been recovered from the Narvik Pinch and Joan was asked to be the 'guinea-pig', tasked with using that chapter to re-examine the recovered data in order to test the veracity of Turing's explanation.

The prototype *Bombe* would have continued to be only of limited use unless a way could be found to significantly improve its performance. Gordon Welchman, running Hut 6, realised that the symmetry of each pair of *Steckerbrett* letters could provide a new way of deriving conclusions from an initial *Steckerbrett* hypothesis. Turing was urgently seeking a method for 'simultaneous scanning', rather than the serial method, and realised that Welchman's diagonal board could provide the answer. The diagonal board was incorporated into the design of the Mk II machine being built at Letchworth and, once its value was proven, retro-engineered into the Mk I machine.

Despite the improvement in speed by the introduction of the diagonal board, the team in Hut 8 was not able to make significant progress during the second half of 1940, therefore many of the general staff were made available to decipher intercepted traffic from the German railway authorities. This was a relatively straightforward task as the version of *Enigma* used was very similar to the commercial machine that had been sold commercially before the war.

The results from breaking and reading German railway traffic were of most use to Military Intelligence in Hut 5, under the command of John Tiltman, as the plain text revealed detailed timetables which then enabled the Royal Air Force to mount bombing raids with some expectation of doing real damage. The 'big room' worked on the German railway transmits until the end of the winter, when more information on the naval *Enigma* became available to the cryptanalysts.

The Battle of Britain continued through 1940 and the bombing continued to disrupt everyday life. At Bletchley Park the rules concerning evacuation of personnel to the shelters were relaxed; compulsory evacuation being delayed until the 'Red Alert' was signaled, and only then at the 'discretion' of the individuals concerned. Bletchley Park's greatest defence, however, was in the maintenance of security and that the existence of the facility remained unknown among the general public or even the military, except on a 'need to know' basis.

With just one day off each week, Joan, like others, was not able to go home to her parents in Dulwich for more than a day trip. At Christmas 1940 travel freedoms were even more restricted than normal and so the season was spent in very much the same way as the rest of the year.

Even within Bletchley Park, the breaking of *Enigma* was not widely known and a highly secret visit by a four-man American delegation was kept in the dark during their February 1941 visit.

> The four Americans left no chronology or log of their time at Bletchley Park. Nevertheless, it is possible to reconstruct some of the time line of their stay from their surviving oral histories and correspondence. However, this approach yields no more than the periods at which they are most likely to have been away from the British code breaking center visiting other sites. There is one exception, and this is the date when the decision was made in London to disclose Bletchley Park's success against the *Enigma* and the workings of the *Bombe*, a decision which was reached in late February and implemented in early March. It therefore seems likely that most discussions not involving the *Enigma* -

which, as stated earlier, the British initially had placed off the agenda - would have occurred before that time, with those related to it invariably coming after[17].

The American delegation was made up of two navy men, Robert Weeks and Prescott Currier, and two from the army, Abraham Sinkov and Leo Rosen. The delegation brought with them cryptographic equipment and documentation centred, largely, on the breaking of Italian and Japanese codes. The delegation travelled from Chesapeake Bay to Scapa Flow, on the battleship HMS *King George V*, transferring to the cruiser HMS *Neptune* for the journey to Sheerness, and then by car to London.

The American itinerary had not been pre-specified and their visit to Bletchley Park was something of a surprise to them. They were installed at Shenley Park, close to Bletchley, the estate of Lord John Cadman, the then president of the Anglo-Persian Oil Company. The Cadmans were not informed of the reasons for the visit, but saw their visitors leave each morning after breakfast, returning each evening for dinner with their hosts.

> AUTHOR'S NOTE: *A memorandum to Churchill reported that the Chiefs of Staff felt that the progress made in probing the German Armed Forces cryptography should be shared with the Americans, but only the technical aspects, not the results. Ultra intelligence was to remain a closely guarded secret.*

The Americans sailed from Greenock on the 24th March on board HMS *Revenge* bound for Halifax, Nova Scotia; transferring to USS *Overton* to take them to Washington. The disclosure to the American delegation that Bletchley Park was able to break, to some extent, the *Enigma* code was the start of a substantial change in the relationship between the security services of both sides. However, some technical information was also held back, notably the extent of Britain's success in breaking Japanese codes.

Chapter 7

Operation Claymore

In early 1941, Winston Churchill was very aware of the need to force Hitler to spread his troops out as thinly as possible along the vast Atlantic coast, which Germany sought to control. From the Artic coast of Norway to the mountains of the Pyrenees, every soldier guarding a remote beach or port was one less soldier preparing to mount an attack on Kent from the Pas-de-Calais. The more remote and inhospitable the German outposts, and the longer and more difficult the supply chain, the more German military morale would suffer.

Churchill saw Norway as Hitler's most vulnerable coastal location. An attack on Norway, into the Artic Circle would be the hardest to repel, would be at the very extreme of German supply routes, and would force the enemy to commit very many unhappy and dissatisfied troops to reinforce the entire coast. More than simply striking a blow against the enemy, an attack on Norway would boost public morale at home, a public still smarting from the German invasion of Norway a year earlier. An effective retaliation would confirm his own position as Prime Minister, specifically after Neville Chamberlain's defeat in consequence of the German invasion and his ineffectual attempts to dismiss them.

A large-scale commando raid was planned for the Lofoten Islands, an archipelago, stretching out into the North Atlantic off the west coast of Norway.

> As far as the commandos taking part in the operation were concerned, it was merely a diversionary raid, one of the morale-boosting attacks favoured by Winston Churchill who, notwithstanding Britain's stretched resources, wanted to take the fight to the Germans, thereby forcing them to leave extra troops in Norway. Fuel tanks and fish factories were to be hit, German ships were to be sunk and Norwegian collaborators captured. Then the commandos were to withdraw[18].

Planning for Operation Claymore began in late February, led by Captain Clifford Caslon who was the commanding officer of the destroyer HMS *Somali*. The flotilla of five destroyers and two troop carriers left Scapa Flow heading north for the Faeroes where they refuelled, and then continued north, turning due east towards Norway, arriving at the Lofoten Islands, inside the Artic Circle, in the early hours of the morning of 4th March.

The landing of the two hundred and fifty commandoes were virtually unopposed, the only shots fired being from the armed trawler *Krebs*; fire was returned and *Krebs* began sinking. The ammunition store had taken a direct hit, the boiler room had exploded and the stricken vessel was abandoned with the crew taking to the water. The commander of the *Krebs*, Lieutenant Hans Kupfinger, had thrown his *Enigma* machine overboard before he was killed but had not been able to do the same with the code books.

The *Krebs* stranded on a half-submerged flat rock, rather than sinking into deep water, so when HMS *Somali* returned she put out a boarding party which rescued some spare *Enigma* rotor wheels, and a set of code books containing the German 'Home Waters' keys for February. In addition they brought back the *Kriegsmarine* gridded chart of northern European waters, valuable because Germany identified ship positions by grid locations rather than by latitude and longitude.

Operation Claymore was successful in all aspects of its primary goals; 800,000 gallons of fish oil was destroyed, by burning, two hundred and twenty-eight prisoners of war were taken, and eighteen thousand tons of shipping sunk. The returning naval force also brought back three hundred Norwegian volunteers for the Free Norwegian forces operating out of Britain. The destruction of fish oil was not entirely inconsequential to the enemy in as much as, transported back to Germany, glycerine was extracted, a vital ingredient in the manufacture of high explosives.

Armed with the booty from Operation Claymore, Joan and the other Seniors in Hut 8 were able to read the whole of German naval traffic for February, albeit some weeks behind actual events, but the retrospective analysis of such information revealed valuable information. One such reveal enabled the capture of two German weather ships, the first *München* on 7th May, the second *Lauenburg* on 28th June; both captures resulted in code books being recovered and sent straight back to Bletchley.

The weather ships were converted fishing vessels, fitted with additional water tanks and reserve fuel bunkers for longer periods at sea than in fishing mode; they also carried 150-watt transmitters, 40-watt portable transmitters and various receivers. They were crewed with a mix of civilians and military and were armed only for self-protection, everyone on board was dressed in mufti but wore *Deutsche Wehrmacht* armbands Most significantly all the ships carried *Enigma* machines for reporting weather observations.

The *München* received orders to take up station three hundred miles east of Iceland, sailing from Trondheim on the 1st May, carrying the cipher keys for both May and June in case the expected twenty-five day duty was extended. Harry Hinsley, a Bletchley Park analyst working in Hut 4, proposed that the undefended *München* be attacked with the object of recovering the key books. Three British cruisers and four destroyers swept grid square AE39 for the German weather ship and found her late in the afternoon of 7th May; the British flotilla rained down shells and the weather ship's crew began to abandon ship, without attempting to scuttle her.

The boarding party recovered fewer papers than they had hoped, but amongst them were the Short Weather Cipher and the home waters *Enigma* keys for June. A deliberately misleading British communiqué to the effect that the *München* had been fired upon and sunk, while in fact she had been taken as a prize, served to preserve the German belief that *Enigma* had not been compromised. To maintain the deception a British communiqué casually referred to the incident noting that an armed German trawler had been scuttled before it could be boarded.

Harry Hinsley was not a mathematician but had won a scholarship to St John's, Cambridge to read history. He had been recruited by Alastair Denniston in July 1939 but had spent the summer visiting his girlfriend in the German city of Koblenz, but had left in a hurry, crossing the border into Switzerland just before war was declared. He immediately reported to Bletchley Park, joining Hut 4, working on the interpretation and dissemination of naval Enigma decrypts.

Fired with success, Harry Hinsley searched German traffic for a second weather ship to attack, and identified the *Lauenburg* as a likely target. He speculated that, having left Trondheim during the last few days of May she might well have the key books for the whole of June and July and be heading to grid square AB72, an area used by previous weather ships. Hinsley's thinking suggested that although the current code books may be with the *Enigma* machine and be jettisoned at the approach of a British warship, the following month's code books would be kept in a safe and, perhaps overlooked, in the panic.

The *Lauenburg* took up station north-east of Iceland, and about three hundred miles inside the Artic Circle, amid the icebergs breaking free from off the shores of Greenland.

A force of one cruiser and three destroyers formed the attack flotilla and swept the target grid square looking for the weather ship. Just before seven o'clock on the evening of 28th June the destroyer HMS *Tartar* found the *Lauenburg* coming out from behind a large iceberg. The order was given to open fire on the weather ship but not to strike her and so endanger the material that was requested by Bletchley Park.

Other ships of the flotilla, with the same orders regarding direct hits, began firing. All but two of the German crew took to the lifeboats, leaving two men behind to throw the *Enigma* overboard and try to burn as much paperwork as possible in the ship's boiler. The boarding party met no opposition but found papers strewn all across the wheelhouse and charthouse. Thirteen mailbags full of paperwork was retrieved and transferred to *Tartar* where the GC&CS representative Allon Bacon, who had sailed with the flotilla, examined and sorted it ready to be shipped back to Bletchley Park.

Although *Lauenburg* was a new ship and in good order it was decided that she should be sunk, rather that taken back as a prize lest she were spotted and that it were thought that the security of *Enigma* had been compromised. By nine o'clock that evening the weather ship and, as far as the Germans knew, all her secret equipment and papers were lying in a thousand fathoms of water. Two days later Allon Bacon transferred to the *Dunluce Castle* at Scapa Flow to cross to Thurso, then by train to Edinburgh and London; finally to Bletchley Park on 2nd July.

An inquiry into the loss of the *Lauenburg* conducted by the Kriegsmarine concluded that she was probably compromised by documents seized aboard the tanker *Gedania*, one of the *Bismarck's* supply ships captured by HMS *Marsdale* on 4th June[22].

Only one day's work was lost from the 30th June, when the *München's* codebooks expired, until 2nd July when the *Lauenburg's* codebook came into use.

With a marked improvement in the speed at which decrypts could be handed over to the Admiralty, and then acted upon, there was a danger that Germany would realise that Enigma had been broken, change their procedures and leave Bletchley back in the dark. The most notable British success was in destroying seven out of eight supply ships sent out into the Atlantic ahead of Bismarck; fortunately, the German belief that Enigma was unbreakable led them to blame the British secret service and its army of spies.

The benefits from the successful raids on the *München* and the *Lauenburg* were augmented by the serendipitous capture of *U-110* by HMS *Bulldog*, escorting the British convoy OB318 five days out of Liverpool bound for various North American ports. Just off Greenland, the convoy was spotted by a German submarine that reported her position and was then quickly joined by six other submarines with the intention of attacking the convoy, one of which was *U-110*, under the command of Kapitänleutnant Fritz-Julius Lemp. The escort group picked up *U-110* presence by using ASDIC and immediately attacked the submarine, using depth charges and forcing her to the surface.

As the submarine broke the surface, her conning tower opened, and the first few men poured out onto the deck. Fearing that they were about to turn the stern-mounted cannon on the escort ships, small arms fire was directed at the Germans, killing a number of men. A British Lewis gun briefly joined the small arms fire but was quickly halted, preparing for HMS *Bulldog* to close on the stricken submarine and ready a boarding party. This was to be led by Sub-Lt David Balme who, without the benefit of any instructions as to his task, was simply told to recover all important papers, ciphers, charts – anything that he could find.

The recovered *Enigma* machine and rotors, as well as codebooks and gridded charts were returned to *Bulldog*, and preparations were made to tow *U-110* back to Scapa Flow but there were other submarines still in the area and two of the convoy ships had already been sunk. The remaining ships of the convoy reformed and set of across the Atlantic towards their destination. HMS *Bulldog* set off eastwards with the submarine in tow, making only four knots, increasing only to six knots by the following morning. By midday the submarine had begun to settle in the water and the tow line was axed, allowing her to sink, and *Bulldog* continued on to Scapa Flow.

The recovered material revealed a further refinement to the Germans' use of *Enigma* which took the form of a two stage cipher; enciphering the original signal and then to enciphering again, with different *Enigma* settings, before finally transmitting the message; to be deciphered by the same two-stage process by the receiver. This double encipher process was confined to 'officer-only' signals with their top-secret content, hence the name *Offizierte* signals, a problem which was given over to Joan Clarke to solve.

Joan Clarke included in her team a temporary junior administrative officer by the name of Leslie Yoxall who, like Joan, had been recruited from Cambridge University by Gordon Welchman, although teaching at Manchester Grammar School immediately before Bletchley Park beckoned. The solution lay in using *Banburismus* to determine the probable key settings for further work on the *Bombe*, but despite the introduction of the diagonal board a double encipher was too long a process to be able to break on a regular basis.

Leslie Yoxall came up with a two-stage solution to the problem, decoding a message which consisted of only eighty letters, which was some feat since Alan Turing had prophesied that a message length of at least two hundred characters would be required. Joan Clarke refined the method further by improving the speed of the second stage, so speeding up the entire process; her name however, for some reason, was not attached to the method, and so the entire procedure (*Yoxallismus*) was named after Leslie Yoxall[19].

During the summer of 1941 Winston Churchill paid a visit to Bletchley Park, met with the senior cryptanalysts and generally gave them encouragement, referring to them as "the geese that laid the golden eggs and never cackled". The very existence of Bletchley Park was so secret that Churchill entered through the mansion doors alone, leaving his Principal Private Secretary, John Martin, outside in the car.

> During his visit he tried to walk into Hut 8, where the daily struggle to break the Naval *Enigma* took place, only to find his way barred by Shaun Wylie, one of the senior cryptographers, who was sitting on the floor in front of the door reading a document. Then Churchill tried the next door in the corridor and burst in to find Hugh Alexander, the man who was to take over the administration of the hut from Alan Turing, also sitting on the floor, sorting through piles of papers. Of course, everyone got up when they saw it was the prime minister, but it was clear that Churchill was a little nonplussed by the apparent chaos he had encountered[23].

> This was reflected in the speech which he gave to the Bletchley park workers gathered in front of the house. It began with the words: "To look at you, one would not think you knew anything secret . . ." [24].

In the summer of 1941 the term ULTRA SECRET was introduced for information which had been produced directly from the *Enigma* decrypts; secret reports from Bletchley Park, thereafter, went by the code name ULTRA.

> *AUTHOR'S NOTE: In order to disguise the fact that ULTRA intelligence was the result of breaking the various Enigma codes, the intelligence distributed to Allied units was attributed to a spy operating behind German lines and given the code name Boniface, who was said to control a fictional series of agents throughout Germany.*

The summer of 1941 also marked a significant change to the direction in which the war would progress. Luftwaffe decrypts from Hut 6 pointed to a likely German invasion of the Soviet Union, which actually began 22nd June. As a consequence there was greater emphasis placed on deciphering army intercepts, the war in the Atlantic therefore, taking second place to Operation Barbarossa.

Winston Churchill

(internet image)

As summer changed to autumn, and the focus of urgent attention moved from the Atlantic to the Eastern Front, the Bletchley budget was not keeping up with the work-load; this showed primarily in the number of staff available to operate the *Bombes*. Breaking with protocol Alan Turing, Gordon Welchman, Hugh Alexander and Stuart Milner-Barry wrote directly to Winston Churchill. The letter was dated 21st October, the anniversary of the Battle of Trafalgar, a date that would have resonated with Churchill.

> Our reason for writing to you direct is that for months we have done everything that we possibly can through the normal channels, and that we despair of any early improvement without your intervention. . . it is difficult to bring home to the authorities finally responsible either the importance of what is done here or the urgent necessity of dealing promptly with our requests. . . Owing to shortage of staff and the overworking of his present team the Hollerith section here under Mr Freeborn has had to stop working night shifts. The effect of this is that the finding of the naval keys is being delayed at least twelve hours every day. A further serious danger now threatening us is that some of the skilled male staff, both with the British Tabulating Company at Letchworth . . . who have so far been exempt from military service, are now liable to be called up.

We have written this letter entirely on our own initiative. We do not know who or what is responsible for our difficulties, and most emphatically we do not want to be taken as criticising Commander Travis who has all along done his utmost to help us in every possible way. But if we are to do our job as well as it could and should be done it is absolutely vital that our wants, small as they are, should be promptly attended to. We have felt that we should be failing in our duty if we did not draw your attention to the facts and to the effects that they are having and must continue to have on our work, unless immediate action is taken.

The result was immediate; an 'Action This Day' instruction was issued by Churchill and handed to General Ismay:

Make sure they have all they want on extreme priority and report to me that this has been done.

The Japanese attack on Pearl Harbour and Germany's declaration of war on the United States, while strengthening the hope of eventual victory had the immediate effect of withdrawing American naval vessels from the Atlantic, where they had been protecting the Atlantic convoys, into the Pacific theatre of war. With U-boats still operating off the Eastern seaboard of America, shipping losses increased dramatically.

Shipping losses were aggravated by America's refusal to introduce a blackout along the coast such that the dark outline of individual ships, sailing independently or gathering to form convoys, were silhouetted against illuminated coastal cities; German U-boats were able to lay off-shore and simply pick off their victims with impunity.

Merchant ships continued to use marked routes and show navigation lights. Coastal communities asked to 'consider' turning their illuminations off , but no request was made to the cities.

AUTHOR'S NOTE: American coastal communities resisted the imposition of a blackout because of the potential damage to tourism. American public opinion was not entirely pro-British and was resistant to showing overt signs of support or sympathy for Britain.

This period was dubbed the 'second happy time' by German mariners, when they could attack British mercantile shipping with relative ease. This situation continued for most of 1942 with over six hundred vessels, more that three million tons, destroyed with only twenty-two submarines lost.

CHAPTER 8

THE FOURTH ROTOR AND U-559

On the 1st February 1942 the German Navy introduced a new version of the *Enigma* machine that proved to be as great an obstacle to the Bletchley Park cryptanalysts as had been *Dolphin*, which had marked a significant improvement over the versions in use with the German army and air force. Intercepted traffic began to remain unsolved; *Banburismus* produced no viable keys with which to use the *Bombes*, and existing manual methods yielded no results. Joan Clarke and others in Hut 8 calculated that the Enigma machine must have been modified to incorporate a fourth rotor.

Not all naval traffic was subject to the change as the new version of *Enigma* was introduced only for the ocean-going U-boats. Surface vessels and U-boats operating in coastal waters continued to use the three-wheeled *Enigma* which meant that Bletchley Park was still able to supply decrypts of signals detailing U-boat sailings from home ports and their movements within Axis controlled waters. The vital information of where the U-boats were hunting, their numbers and formations, was suddenly not available and this put the convoys in ever increasing danger.

Germany's introduction of a the fourth wheel immediately had the effect of increasing the number of possible keys by a factor of twenty-six; fortunately the fourth wheel was not included in the automatic stepping system but remained fixed at its original setting. However, without having seen one of the new four-wheel *Enigma* machines, this was not known at Bletchley Park and the worst scenario was feared. In addition to the additional wheel, an extra 'reflector' was also included, which introduced a further complication to the task for Bletchley Park. The new four-rotor *Enigma* was dubbed *Shark* by the cryptanalysts in Hut 8, and much effort went in trying to resolve the problem.

The presence of the fourth wheel and 'reflector' was understood by Joan and her colleagues in Hut 8, but it was really the speed of the *Bombe* which limited its usefulness. It was not feasible to expand the scope of the *Bombe* to include a fourth wheel, not only because of the engineering costs and difficulties, but the speed at which they could operate would have meant a significant increase in the number of *Bombes* needed merely to keep to the existing pace. If there were to be any possibility of significantly speeding up the operation then the electromagnetic relays would need to be replaced by electronics.

During 1942, the work on which Joan Clarke was engaged was a long and frustrating effort to break into the new four-wheel navel *Enigma*, but without sight of the new machine and a detailed knowledge of its workings. Much of the work of Hut 8 was spent in the old-fashioned breaking of codes rather than the more automated approach of 1941, with consequential delays from intercept to solution. From Joan's point of view, sight of the four-wheel *Enigma* was of vital importance, something she was not going to see until the very end of the year.

After Harry Hinsley's success in planning raids on German weather ships during 1941, and Bletchley Park being desperate to have sight of a new four rotor *Enigma*, an attack on Dieppe, codenamed Operation Jubilee, was to have the seizure of one of the new machines included in its list of objectives. One group of commandos was tasked with reaching the local headquarters of the Kriegsmarine and carrying off all German naval cipher machines, code books and secret documents. The prime military objective of the raid was to destroy the shore batteries that threatened British shipping in the Channel[25].

The commandos targeting Kriegsmarine HQ never reached their objective, the raiding force being bogged down on the beach, losing much equipment and many men, mostly Canadians, in the process. Nearly five thousand Canadian soldiers set off for France, less than one thousand returned, many of them wounded. Although the losses were not directly due to the need to capture a four rotor *Enigma*, indirectly the death toll to support the work at Bletchley Park was steadily increasing.

U-boat attacks were not confined to the Atlantic; a number of German submarines were operating in the Mediterranean, keeping free access to the Suez Canal from the Allies and disrupting supplies to the British army in North Africa. By the Autumn of 1942 the number of submarines had reached fifteen, all operating with the four-wheel *Enigma*, an example of which was still to fall into British hands. British ships were constantly on alert because of the U-boat danger, but also for any opportunity which might secure a new four-rotor *Enigma* machine, although the crews were not aware of just how vital such a seizure was to the progress of the war.

U-559 commanded by Kapitänleutnant Hans Heidtmann, was lying mid-way between Port Said and Haifa, with instructions to sail for Messina in Sicily, and to transmit a meteorological report when able. In the early hours of 30th October the submarine surfaced and transmitted its report using the Short Weather Cipher. While it was on the surface, *U-559* was identified by a radar-equipped Sunderland flying boat on patrol above the convoy route, which ran between Port Said and the British naval base at Haifa.

> *AUTHOR'S NOTE: The Sunderland flying boat patrol bomber was developed as a long-range patrol/reconnaissance aircraft armed with machine guns, aerial mines, and depth charges. It also carried searchlights and detection radar.*

Five British destroyers were promptly dispatched to the area with instructions to locate and destroy the submarine; arriving just after noon they sighted the submarine's periscope retreating below the surface. However, in the clear waters of the Mediterranean, the submerged submarine could be seen by a second, observation aeroplane, which had been dispatched to the scene; it guided the destroyers to the target area where *U-559* was lying in deep water.

HMS *Pakenham* was the first to make contact, with HMS *Petard* and HMS *Dulverton* each dropping patterns of depth charges. With no immediate results the attack continued on through the day, but it was not until nearly eleven in the evening that *U-559* broke the surface. The continuous pounding from the surface craft had fractured the outer skin and water had begun to flood into the submarine, such that it was lying with its stern lower than its bows. The carbon dioxide level had been rising steadily, causing nausea, and the pressurised air was leaking out into the water.

As the submarine broke the surface she was illuminated by the searchlights of HMS *Hurworth* and HMS *Petard*, and strafed by their guns. As well as the damage from the depth charges the strafing had holed the submarine such that she was slowly sinking as the crew abandoned ship and began swimming towards the British destroyers. The small group, left behind to scuttle the submarine before they also abandoned ship, were in such haste that they managed to bend the lever mechanisms that controlled the vents and so thwarted the procedure to sink the four wheel *Enigma* machine and its code books.

Lt Commander Mark Thornton, commanding HMS *Petard*, brought his ship as close to the submarine as possible while a boarding party prepared to claim the submarine. There was no time to launch the ship's whaler for the boarding party, so it was a matter of taking to the water. Colin Grazier, an able seaman, and First Lt Anthony Fasson jumped from the *Petard* and began to swim towards the stricken craft, being joined by a fifteen year old (under aged) canteen assistant, Tommy Brown. All three men reached the submarine and went below, via the conning tower, retrieving books and papers from the sinking U-boat.

Tommy Brown, pictured later, on joining the Navy

(internet image)

The whaler, under the command of Gordon Connell was launched and began to take on the material being retrieved from the sinking submarine. They also pulled some of the Germans from the sea who sat amid the recovered equipment and code books. Grazier and Fasson went down the conning tower many times, Tommy Brown receiving the recovered material and passing it to the whaler; the submarine all the time sinking lower and lower in the water. Connell instructed the three men to leave the submarine and swim to the whaler.

> The seas were breaking continuously over the remaining portion of the hull that remained visible, the conning tower, and water was pouring out through the shell holes. It was a crazy scene, brilliantly illuminated by the slowly circling destroyer that continued to try to give a lee to the stricken and now obviously sinking submarine. There were cries from drowning crew members, and a number still clung to the side of the whaler as we struggled to hold the sea-boat alongside the conning tower and at the same time keep afloat. As I was about to jump into the sea and clamber onto the tower, it quite suddenly disappeared, leaving nothing to be seem above the breaking waves. We yelled and called out the names of our shipmates. Only Tommy responded, his head bobbling up almost alongside the sea-boat[26].

Grazier and Fasson were both drowned when *U-559* finally sank; Tommy Brown escaped and was taken back to HMS *Petard*. The recovered papers were taken to Haifa, to be handed over to naval intelligence officers for onward shipment to Bletchley Park for analysis. Again, men had shown great bravery in order to retrieve information, the value of which was entirely unknown to them; two men had lost their lives: two posthumous George Crosses were awarded. Tommy Brown, as a civilian, received the George Medal but his age meant that he was then banned from service at sea and confined to shore duties, still with the NAAFI, but promoted to Senior Canteen Assistant.

> *AUTHOR'S NOTE: Once Tommy Brown's true age became known to the authorities, he was released from serving on HMS Petard, but not from the NAAFI, and continued to work on shore, promoted to Senior Canteen Assistant. He later returned to sea, at full age, on board HMS Belfast but while on leave in 1945 he was killed attempting to rescue his young sister from a fire at the family home in South Shields.*

Joan Clarke, in Hut 8, first began working on the *U-559* 'pinch' toward the end of November and within the following two weeks made the discovery that the fourth-wheel added a much lower level of complexity than had been anticipated and that the ocean going U-boat codes were identical to the previous three-wheel codes for any given day with simply another letter added; the fourth wheel position was passive, without employing the complexity of the other three.

Having determined the three rotors the fourth had only to be tested in twenty-six positions, the possible combinations being (26x26x26)+26 = 17,602, rather than the feared 26x26x26x26 = 456,976 had the fourth rotor been fully integrated, as were the other three. Although the task was significantly more complex and time consuming than the previous three rotor *Enigma*, the solution could again be partially assisted by the *Bombes* which were increasingly available. Hut 8 began reading and decrypting U-boat Atlantic transmissions again. The location of wolf packs were charted and then hunted down. Allied shipping losses began to fall as 1943 dawned.

Joan was fully employed with maximising the intelligence that had been gained from the sinking *U-559*. Alan Turing was aboard the *Queen Elizabeth* bound for Washington, via New York, in an attempt to resolve some of the tensions between the British and American intelligence services. With Alan Turing in America, and expected to be absent a few months, Hugh Alexander became *de facto* head of Hut 8 without any formal recognition of the fact. During this time *Enigma* work was moving operations to the newly completed 'Block D', somewhat further away from the Mansion and day-to-day supervision.

The decision to construct 'Block D' was reached with multiple purposes in mind. The number of people working at Bletchley Park was continuing to increase, not only in Huts 8 and 6 but throughout the site, and further accommodation was required to house them. The new building was constructed with a view to protecting the men and women who were to work there, and the materials that were so vital to the war effort, and offered a greater degree of protection. The construction was designed by the Ministry of Works and Buildings (MOWB) following their standard 'spider block' pattern, comprising thirteen office spurs, opening off a central spine corridor, and designed to accommodate five hundred and thirty.

Fletton brickwork in English bond (external walls) and stretcher bond (internal walls), mostly erected with a reinforced-concrete frame and concrete-slab roof, but with two steel-framed compartments at the southern end of Spurs H and K which had special functions (teleprinter rooms). White-painted brickwork. Metal windows, mainly of 4 x 4 rectangular panes, with red-tile sills. Slightly pitched roof of reinforced concrete slabs[27].

This was an opportunity to house all the departments that were involved in the breaking of *Enigma* under one roof, releasing the wooden huts for other purposes. The personnel from Hut 8 (naval), Hut 6 (army and air-force) and Hut 3, Hut 4 moving to 'Block A' (dissemination of Enigma decoded traffic) were all moved to the new building, the design of which meant that it was still possible to minimise 'cross contamination' between departments thus maintaining an important security measure.

The move into 'Block D' meant that the cryptanalysts of Hut 6 and 8 had a little more contact with one another and with personnel in Huts 3 and 4 and thus Joan would have come into contact with John Cairncross, later to be identified as the 'fifth' man to Philby, Maclean, Burgess and Blunt, the Cambridge spies. Cairncross, a fluent German speaker, had studied modern languages at Trinity College and had already been working for the Foreign Office before being transferred to Bletchley Park.

Despite the move from the old wooden huts to the new secure brick and concrete block, the names of the departments were kept the same as those by which they had been previously known; thus Joan Clarke continued to be associated with the department named Hut 8.

The 'Holden Understanding' of the previous year, and the introduction of the US four-wheel *Bombes* manufactured by NCR in Ohio, meant a closer liaison between Bletchley Park and the US Navy's signals intelligence and cryptanalysis group (Op-20-G) based at Mount Vernon in Washington DC, in a building which had once been a girl's school. American personnel began working alongside the British in the new Block D and one made a quite complimentary assessment of their acceptance at Bletchley.

My official duty was to report back to Washington what was happening at Bletchley Park. But this was not a full-time job, so I undertook to be a cryptanalyst while I was there . . . very noticeable that people there took a personal interest in their work . . . there were lots of academics there, particularly from Cambridge. I met professorial types on an equal footing in a way I would never have otherwise done. They were always a level or two above me. I found their attitude towards life very interesting. They were academics primarily and their personal life was secondary[28].

The US Navy *Bombes* used drums for the *Enigma* rotors in much the same way as the British *Bombes* but with eight *Enigma* equivalents on the front and eight on the back. The fast drum rotated at thirty-four times the speed of the early British *Bombes* and 'stops' were detected electronically and details automatically printed before restarting. The running time for a four-rotor run was about twenty minutes, and for a three-rotor run, about fifty seconds.

When the Americans began to turn out *Bombes* in large numbers there was a constant interchange of signal - cribs, keys, message texts, cryptographic chat and so on. This all went by cable being first enciphered on the combined Anglo-American cipher machine, C.C.M. Most of the cribs being of operational urgency rapid and efficient communication was essential and a high standard was reached on this; an emergency priority signal consisting of a long crib with crib and message text repeated as a safeguard against corruption would take under an hour from the time we began to write the signal out in Hut 8 to the completion of its deciphering in Op-20-G. As a result of this we were able to use the Op-20-G *Bombes* almost as conveniently as if they had been at one of our outstations twenty or thirty miles away[29].

With the improvement in speed, and an increase in the number of *Bombes* available, less emphasis was placed on the *Banburismus* process which had been relied upon to reduce the number of possibilities of wheel order, thus reducing the amount of time that the *Bombes* would need in order to find the wheel order. Greater success in the fight against the U-boats meant, that by the end of May, the much-depleted Wolf Packs were withdrawn from the Atlantic for re-deployment in the Mediterranean.

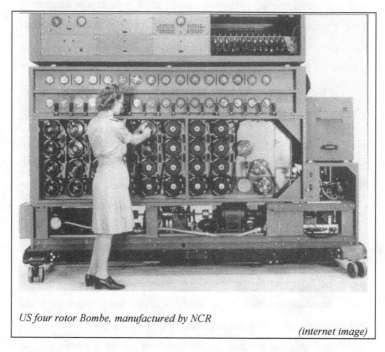

US four rotor Bombe, manufactured by NCR

(internet image)

Hut 8 continued to break the German codes during the remainder of 1943, allowing the almost unhindered shipment of men and materials from America, for the eventual invasion of the European mainland. Germany turned her attention in the northern seas and to the Russian convoys, which were, in the main, the targets of surface craft. The major prize for the British came right at the end of the year with the sinking of the German battleship *Scharnhorst* at the Battle of the North Cape.

A series of *Offizierte* signals had indicated that *Scharnhorst*, at anchor in Altenfjord in northern Norway, was being got ready for sea but, with the delay caused by breaking the double encryption of *Offizierte* signals, the information could not be distributed in time to attack her at anchor. On the afternoon of Christmas day a message from *Scharnhorst* was decrypted by Hut 8: "*Scharnhorst* will pass outward bound as from 1800. Act in accordance with today's written instructions". *Scharnhorst's* quarry was convoy JW55B comprising nineteen merchant ships, sailing from Loch Ewe in the north west of Scotland to northern Soviet ports.

The British Home Fleet closed on the German Battleship, which was strongly attacked by HMS *Duke of York* and was eventually sunk by a mixture of gunfire and torpedoes at around 9:45pm on the evening of Boxing Day. The decryption of *Offizierte* signals in Hut 8 had played a pivotal role in the attack but had shown the weakness inherent in the changing of *Enigma* codes over the midnight hours, and the time taken to break the encryption in the early hours.

> All but thirty-six of her two thousand strong crew perished in the freezing Artic waters. The captain and commander of *Scharnhorst* were both seen in the water . . . The Captain was dead before he could be reached; the Commander grasped a life-line, but succumbed before he could be hauled in[30].

Thankfully, the main body of naval signals was still being sent in single encrypted *Shark* format rather than in *Offizierte* format and routine decryption could still be achieved in a timely manner.

CHAPTER 9

OPERATION OVERLORD

The main focus of activity for Hut 8 during the first half of 1944 was to support the preparations for the invasion of Europe planned to take place in June of that year. Weather forecasting was vital to the success or failure of the D-Day invasion and coded weather reports from German U-boats, decrypted at Bletchley Park, were a priority as June approached. Communication between Bletchley Park and the Dunstable Meteorological Centre was mainly by motorcycle dispatch riders carrying raw intercepts, once the daily keys had been established by Hut 8, for actual decoding by local staff.

Dunstable Meteorological Centre

(internet image)

Three or four times a day, couriers on motorbikes sped from Bletchley to Dunstable carrying thin cards bearing intercepted German weather codes stripped of their Enigma cipher. At Dunstable, a team of cryptanalysts would further decode the German reports and pass the data on to meteorologists who would plot in on charts. While at first it took days to decipher a message, by 1944 only a few hours or less were usually required[31].

George Cunliffe McVittie was the head of the meteorological section at Bletchley Park, based in Hut 10, which was generally concerned with obtaining continuous information about weather conditions over enemy-held territory. The information gained was used largely to provide information in support of Allied bombing raids but, as the planning for an invasion of Europe progressed, the army took more and more interest in the results. Also, the number of SOE operations increased with low-level weather conditions becoming of greater concern with the increasing number of three-man teams being dropped into various parts of France as part of Operation *Jedburgh*, in order to launch widespread acts of resistance prior to D-day.

> *AUTHOR'S NOTE: Operation Jedburgh was intended to demonstrate overt resistance activity behind enemy lines during the run-up to D-Day. Jedburgh teams normally parachuted into occupied territory by night to meet with local resistance groups. Their main function was to provide a link with the Allied forces and arrange airdrops of arms and ammunition.*

McVittie, again from Kings College, Cambridge, began the meteorological section at Bletchley Park single-handed at the outbreak of war in 1939. He had worked closely with Hut 8 from the very beginning, interpreting the intercepted weather signals from German submarines and weather ships. His work with the RAF at Leighton Buzzard and with the Meteorological Office in Dunstable proved so successful that by the end of 1943 the section employed sixty people. The introduction of the four-rotor *Enigma* had severely impacted Atlantic meteorology, but Joan's breakthrough on *Shark* had happened in time for the 1944 initiative.

> McVittie became a weatherman by accident. As he told David DeVorkin during an oral history interview in 1978, he registered with the Royal Society "to do whatever one thought one could do, if a war did come on . . . There was obviously not going to be any astronomy involved in the war – not in 1938 – so I put myself down to do meteorological work. Not that I knew any meteorology. Not that I knew anything about it, but it seemed the nearest approach to do what I did

know about. And so, indeed it proved to be. Except of course that what
I did eventually get involved in was not mathematical meteorology, but
reading Hitler's correspondence[32].

While the cryptanalysts in Huts 6 and 8 were continuing with their work on *Enigma*, elsewhere in Bletchley Park there were others wrestling with the *Lorenz* code employed by Berlin to communicate with German army commanders in the field. The methodology was totally different from that of *Enigma*, working instead on streams of data encrypted using Boolean logic (XOR) which gave a significant improvement in security and in transmission speed as compared to *Enigma* which had to be sent via Morse Code. *Lorenz* was linked directly to a teleprinter machine and input was streamed very fast from pre-punched paper tape. Not the least of Bletchley Park's problems was that nobody had seen the transmitter or receiver, so all the work on breaking the code was undertaken 'blind'.

The solution was in the development of the *Colossus* computer, programmed via plug board rather than stored program, built by Tommy Flowers, of the Dollis Hill Post Office Research Station, using algorithms developed at Bletchley Park by Bill Tutte and his team of mathematicians. By an incredible effort, the first Colossus was installed and working five days before the Normandy landings; a credit to Tommy Flowers and to Bill Tutte, another product of Trinity College, Cambridge and a contemporary of Joan Clarke.

In the days immediately before D-Day higher security than normal was imposed on those working at Bletchley Park; they were confined to site, sleeping as best they could, eating in their office or at their place of work, and not being permitted to socialise with anyone but their immediate colleagues. Although staff, generally, did not know the details or exact date for the invasion, the majority of the work force were aware that some major event was imminent. Heads of the main sections, who would have to accommodate the extra work load that would inevitably follow the D-day landings, were briefed, and this included the Seniors in Hut 8.

For codebreaker Harry Hinsley, D-Day involved him sitting firm
behind his desk for over twenty-four hours. The climax was marked by

an important telephone call from Downing Street. First a woman asked him to confirm that he was Mr Hinsley, then he heard Churchill's voice asking: "Has the enemy heard that we are coming yet?" Hinsley assured the Prime Minister that the first Bletchley decrypts of German messages were coming on the teleprinter. A couple of hours later, Churchill called Hinsley again: "How's it going? Is anything happening yet?"[33]

Although the Germans may not have known the exact date or location of the D-Day landings the events of 6th June 1944 were not entirely unexpected. There was a considerable threat from U-Boats attacking the British and American armada that crossed the Channel, and patrolling submarines were the most likely source of early warning, lying on the bottom during the day and on the surface overnight. In anticipation, extra radio intercept stations were set up within Bletchley Park in order to maximize the speed of response to any indication of danger to the invasion force. There were some doubts about the wisdom of erecting a sea of radio masts, advertising Bletchley Park's existence, but it was concluded that being able to pass on *Enigma* decrypts to the naval escorts within thirty minutes of intercept made it a justified risk.

Hut 18 was actually fitted out as a Y-Station and, in anticipation of Wrens and WAAFs being on continuous duty during the D-Day period, efforts were made to ensure that sufficient stocks of chocolate, soap and cigarettes were on hand; even an electric iron for the girls to keep their collars and flannels in good order over the coming 'emergency period'. The work of the Wrens was well appreciated, not least by Frank Birch, head of the Naval Section:

> I have been much impressed by the zeal shown by the Wren Assistants carrying intercepts from Hut 18. They are astonishingly quick off the mark and you know this has made a great difference to the time at which Admiralty and Allied Naval Command Expeditionary Force receive information from us, which in its turn must have considerable effect on operations. Would you please congratulate them and thank them from me[34].

As Allied forces secured their foothold in Normandy and then prepared to move east towards the German border, Bletchley Park continued its work unabated. Invasion of Britain became less likely than before and some of the wartime restrictions were relaxed, to the relief of the civilian population both inside and outside Bletchley Park but, not so much for the military staff stationed there. However heavy German bombing continued and growing numbers of V1 (doodlebugs or flying bombs) continued to be directed towards southern England.

U-505 under the command of Oberleutnant Lange left Lorient in March to patrol the western coast of Africa looking for Allied shipping to attack but Hut 8 had been breaking naval Enigma signals and had been tracking the submarine, diverting all Allied shipping away from her. At the end of May, on board the submarine, Lange decided to return to Lorient; *U-505* was short of fuel, her crew frustrated, and their spirits low. Bletchley Park was fully aware that *U-505* was returning to France and also had a good idea of the course he was taking. Hut 4 passed this information along to the Americans who were operating in that area.

> *AUTHOR'S NOTE: The town of Lorient, on the Brittany coast, was home to the German submarine base of Keroman, capable of sheltering thirty submarines under cover. The base was the target of heavy Allied bombing, sustaining substantial damage, but survived through to the end of the war.*

Two days before the D-Day landings the American aircraft carrier USS *Guadalcanal* was leading a task force of five destroyers off the coast of West Africa one of whom, USS *Chatelain,* located a U-Boat on its SONAR and proceeded to attack using *hedgehogs*, which threw multiple spigot mortars forward, to explode on contact with a submarine's hull. This was quickly followed by a pattern of depth charges which resulted in *U-505* being forced to the surface, but fired a torpedo towards *Chatelain* as she did so, to which *Chatelain* replied in kind. As the submarine broke the surface she came under heavy machine gun fire.

USS *Pillsbury* immediately sent out a boarding party, which concentrated on recovering the codebooks and any other documents that they could find. Others concentrated on replacing the cap to the open valve in order to stem the flood of

86

seawater entering the stricken craft. Captain Daniel Gallery, commanding the task force, made the decision to take *U-505* in tow, rather than to sink her. After dismissing Casablanca in Morocco and Dakar in Senegal as suitable destinations he decided to tow the captured submarine to Bermuda; a decision that both Washington and London considered reckless in that it compromised the *Enigma* secret.

On reaching Bermuda, she was impounded and intensively studied by US Navy intelligence. The greatest concern was that the capture of the submarine and of her codebooks should not become known to the Germans. In order that she was assumed to have been sunk rather than captured, she was painted to look like a US submarine and renamed as the USS *Nemo*. The entire crew of *U-505*, being aware of the capture, were detained in isolation from all other prisoners of war, not even being allowed access to the Red Cross, despite the provisions of the Geneva Convention.

> *AUTHOR'S NOTE: The submarine U-505 was donated to the Museum of Science and Industry in Chicago. The inside of the submarine had been stripped out while still held in Bermuda, but was restored by the German companies that had originally fitted her out in 1941.*

The recovered codebooks were handed over to Bletchley Park on 20th June and found to contain the Offizier and regular *Enigma* settings for June 1944, the short weather codebooks, new versions of the bigram tables and short signal which were to come into effect in July and August.

> The 'address book' containing the code used by the U-boats to convert references on the grid chart . . . was also picked up . . . capture of this document meant that for the first time since the positions on the German charts had been encoded, the staff working in the submarine tracking rooms in London and Washington were able to understand immediately the references to locations mentioned in decrypted Enigma messages[35].

Again, Hut 8 was to have a change of leadership; Hugh Alexander moved over to join the effort to break the Japanese codes and was replaced by his junior, Patrick Mahon who had been transferred to Hut 8 during attempts to break the *Shark* code. In recognition of the tremendous effort and contribution she had made to Hut 8, and to the breaking of the naval *Enigma*, Joan Clarke was made deputy head, although her wage rate still failed to match that of her male counterparts. The two other male cryptanalysts who remained, Rolf Noskwith and Richard Pendered, worked alongside Joan without demure.

Hut 8, now with only four cryptanalysts working on the naval *Enigma*, but supported by a large number of others in the 'Big Room' , still managed to maintain a full three shift system. With the necessity for regular time off this put an extraordinary strain on the four Seniors who were, alone, keeping abreast of the naval *Enigma*.

VE Day celebrations

(internet image)

On 8th May 1945 Joan Clarke, along with others at Bletchley Park, celebrated VE Day, but not in Trafalgar Square or outside Buckingham Palace with the crowds. Bletchley Park was still at war. German hostilities had ceased, but the Allies were still fighting Japan, and the Americans needed, and deserved, continuing support in the Pacific.

> We, and our American allies, are still at war with Japan, and we are faced with great responsibilities arising out of the preliminaries to peace in Europe. At some future time we may be called upon again to use the same methods. It is therefore as vital as ever not to relax from

the high standard of security that we have hitherto maintained. The temptation now to 'own up' to our friends and families as to what our work has been is a very real and naturel one. It must be resisted absolutely[36].

However, for twenty-four hours Bletchley Park celebrated:

> After the German surrender, Bletchley Park put on a terrific VE party, a fancy dress ball with oceans to drink, a top band, our own cabaret, special décor, soft lights, and all the trimmings. It must have been quite one of the best end-of-war parties, almost as good as VJ in the Friendly Islands[37].

In the August of 1945 two American B-21s dropped atomic bombs on Japanese cities, the first on Hiroshima and the second on Nagasaki, resulting in Japan's unconditional surrender. The effect upon Stalin of America's bombing of Hiroshima and Nagasaki was dramatic, ordering that the Politburo should take immediate control of the Soviet atomic bomb project. Decryption work within GC&CS increased rapidly as Soviet diplomatic and espionage traffic grew following Stalin's appointment of Lavrentiy Beria to run the entire Soviet atomic project.

The operations which had been the primary activity at Bletchley, and were to continue through the post-war years, were to transfer to Eastcote in north-west London in the borough of Hillingdon but, although referred to variously as RAF Eastcote, RAF Lime Grove and HMS Pembroke it was simply a collection of huts and single story buildings; a mixture of offices and accommodation blocks, the new arrivals living in areas which had previously accommodated some one-hundred *Bombes* as Outstation Eastcote.

With the end of the war, Patrick Mahon was able to make his own assessment on the role that the members of Hut 8 had played and how fortune had been on their side in having time to rise to each challenge as it occurred, the Germans never introducing multiple innovations simultaneously, and so overwhelming the cryptanalysts.

Hut 8's accomplishment consisted in decoding during the course of the war about 1,120,000 messages; the total number of intercepts received was about 1,550,000. It is remarkable that since regular breaking began in the autumn of 1941 the situation has always been under control and no important key has ever ceased to be broken with the exception of Shark between February and December 1942. This continuity of breaking was undoubtedly an essential factor in our success and it does appear to be true to say that if a key has been broken regularly for a long time in the past, it is likely to continue to be broken in the future, provided that no major change in the method of encipherment takes place. This was the great failing of the German cipher authorities and the lesson is clear for anyone concerned with cipher security to read; the Germans introduced their cipher innovations seriatim and gave us time to recover from each blow before delivering the next. The introduction at one fell swoop of all the changes which took place, for example, in 1944 would doubtless have put us out of business but as a result of the methods the Germans adopted we were able to preserve continuity and breaking continued. The developments which were scheduled to take place during the months following the surrender appear alarming, but I believe that we should have survived these also for the same reason. . . while we broke German Naval Ciphers because it was our job to do so and because we believed it to be worth while, we also broke them because the problem was an interesting and amusing one. The work of Hut 8 combined to a remarkable extent a sense of urgency and importance with the pleasure of playing an intellectual game[38].

Following the capitulation of Japan the co-operation between Britain and America on signals intelligence into peacetime was confirmed by both governments, and at a London conference, the following March, an agreement bound Britain, America, Canada, Australia and New Zealand in a mutual intelligence accord with a formal agreement on exchange of material. The UKUSA accord, also known as The Five Eyes

(FVEY), was an extension of the informal British–US Communication Intelligence Agreement (BRUSA) of 1943 to include other English speaking countries.

CHAPTER 10

EASTCOTE GCHQ

The end of the war in the Pacific signalled the end of Bletchley Park and the release of the thousands of personnel who had worked there. Some were simply told that their services were no longer required as they were surplus to requirements; they had their employment terminated on one week's notice and thousands of people walked out through the gates never to return. Others had their departure postponed with a promise that they would be considered for re-employment in other government departments but in the meantime would be involved in de-commissioning Bletchley Park and destroying any evidence of what had taken place there. For those who remained, working patterns reverted to those of peacetime, predominately Monday to Friday with normal working hours. In the later months of 1945 the once-teeming blocks lay empty, the huts sparse of furniture, and many of the rooms in the house empty and echoing. Bletchley was described as a ghost town with just removal men shifting furniture[39].

Joan Clarke, along with others who had proven their worth during the preceding years, were invited to continue working with GC&CS when it relocated from Bletchley Park to its new peacetime location of Eastcote in north-west London[40]. The Soviet threat was well recognised by the Foreign Office and the security services, and the possibility that a similar intellectual effort could be required to combat a future danger had to be planned for. Winston Churchill had been defeated in the July 1945 general election, giving some relief to the fears that the Allies might precipitate in further conflict against Russia, but the Soviet threat was still very real.

GC&CS Eastcote was very much as Bletchley Park had been when Joan first arrived in June 1940, that is, a collection of huts and single story buildings; a mixture of offices and accommodation blocks, the new arrivals working in areas which had previously accommodated some one-hundred *Bombes* when lack of space at Bletchley Park had become a problem. The *Bombes* at Eastcote and those at Bletchley Park were being systematically destroyed in order to hide from the Soviets that Enigma was ever broken, despite the leaks by John Cairncross; the work of Hut 6 and Hut 8 were to remain a secret shared by Britain and the USA only.

Joan with colleagues at Eastcote in March 1946. On the reverse Joan has written 'Bodge, Alan, Self, Colin, Graham'
(courtesy of John Clarke, Joan's nephew)

Joan could have enjoyed a rewarding academic life by returning to Cambridge; her achievements while at Newnham College and her association, even her intellectual parity, with Alan Turing during the war would have ensured her future. For a mathematician of her ability, Cambridge was the obvious choice and would have allowed her to pursue a life of research and of teaching, within a world which her family background would indicate as one to which she was entirely suited.

But Joan had spent five years working in a totally different environment to that of Academia; there were deadlines and frustrations; reliance on the work of others, and colleagues looking to her for results; most significantly the knowledge that lives were at risk and that the security of the nation was something to which she could make a significant contribution. At Bletchley Park she had taken responsibility for her own work and had learnt to direct the work of others; she had experienced a world where she would be judged on her current usefulness rather than her past achievements.

The war proved beyond doubt that the more difficult aspects of our work call for staff of the highest calibre, the successes by the Professors and Dons among our temporary staff, especially perhaps the high grade mathematicians, put that beyond doubt[41].

It is fair to speculate that life for Clarke as a codebreaker had been intensely rewarding in terms of excitement as well as the intellectual thrill of besting the enemy; and that she had no wish to see that excitement end[42].

Hugh Alexander, John Tiltman, Wilfred Bodsworth and Leslie Yoxall also decided to stay on with GC&CS after the war, or at least returned after a short spell elsewhere, as did some others such as Mavis Batey and Margaret Rock who had previously worked for Gordon Welchman in Hut 6. Although all had worked as cryptanalysts at Bletchley, even within Block D, this would be the first time that they had been colleagues in the true sense of the word. The wartime regulations of segregation as a security measure were to be relaxed within the smaller, more collegiate, Eastcote establishment.

The site was split in two by a public footpath: one half of the site located near Lime Grove, consisting of personnel accommodation and administrative services; the other h, protected by military police, was where the code breakers were going to work. The division meant that support personnel, and local residents, could be kept completely unaware of the precise nature of the work taking place in the high security area.

On 1st January 1946 Joan's name appeared in the Civil Division of the New Year Honours list as being appointed a member of the British Empire (MBE) for meritorious service, having been 'employed in a Department of the Foreign Office'; no hint of the true nature of her role was published. Her mother and father, now living in Chichester, were not privy to the secrets that she carried, Joan still being subject to the Official Secrets Act; but they were educated people, and a mathematician of Joan's ability was unlikely to have been awarded an MBE for clerical services.

Although the Labour Government, under Clement Attlee, did not attempt to hide their fears, it was Winston Churchill who found the words and the public stage on which to voice them, and he was able to encapsulate them into a single sentence, from which a two word phrase would galvanise the West.

In March 1946 Winston Churchill, out of office since the previous year's General Election, had been invited to Westminster College in Fulton, Missouri. Intended to rally American public opinion, Churchill shared the stage with President Harry S. Truman, and delivered a speech in which he described the USA as standing at the pinnacle of world power and called for an ever strengthening special relationship between the USA and his own country. Of particular relevance to the cryptanalysts of GC&CS was the threat of the communist 'fifth column' operating clandestinely and communicating back to Moscow in secret.

The words that Churchill spoke at Fulton, Missouri were to become a unifying cry of fear in North America and in Western Europe:

> From Stettin in the Baltic, to Trieste in the Adriatic, an 'Iron Curtain' has descended across the continent. Behind that line lie all the capitals of the ancient states of Central and Eastern Europe. Warsaw, Berlin, Prague, Vienna, Budapest, Belgrade, Bucharest and Sofia; all these famous cities and the populations around them lie in what I must call the Soviet sphere, and all are subject, in one form or another, not only to Soviet influence but to a very high and in some cases increasing measure of control from Moscow.
>
> Nobody knows what Soviet Russia and its Communist international organization intends to do in the immediate future, or what are the limits, if any, to their expansive and proselytizing tendencies.

To find out what the Soviet Union intended to do was the task of the secret services of both Britain and the USA; to read Soviet intelligence traffic was to become the *raison d'etre* for Joan Clarke and her colleagues through the following four decades.

GC&CS Eastcote became fully operational in April 1946 with a change of name to Government Communications Headquarters (GCHQ), although this designation had been used on occasions as a working name for Bletchley Park during the war, it had not been formally adopted. Security was strict, and members of staff who were trying to find lodgings in the area were permitted only to name their place of work as GCHQ, but without giving their landladies any clue as to the work they did. The general population was not to be easily fooled and a place of work, protected by military police, which had been a restricted area during the war, was obviously known to be employed in secret government work.

The first major project at the newly named GCHQ, in which Joan was actively involved, was a joint project with the USA that went by the code-name *Venona* which, like *Ultra*, referred to the intelligence gained, rather than to the methods used, and was based on the vast amount of Soviet traffic that had been intercepted during the war years, and was still being collected, in order to identify active Soviet agents and 'sleepers' operating in government departments. The encryption process involved the use of 'one-time pads' and, until the Soviets made organisational errors, the breaking of the codes relied solely upon the skill and insight of mathematicians.

> *AUTHOR'S NOTE: The Venona project had been started as early as 1943 by American military intelligence who feared that Stalin could sign a separate peace treaty with Germany, thus allowing Germany to release troops from the eastern front to oppose America and Britain in the west.*

Like *Enigma* and *Lorenz*, there were various models of the Soviet enciphered teleprinter system, and GCHQ identified them generically as the *Poets* system, identifying individual machine types as *Coleridge*, *Longfellow* etc. The British had their own collection of intercepted traffic acquired using directional finding equipment, which suggested illicit transmissions from the Soviet Embassy in Kensington Palace Gardens and from other locations in the London area.

The attack on the *Poets* system was led by Hugh Alexander; he headed Section H where Joan Clarke worked. The cryptanalysts at GCHQ, able to draw upon the enormous computer power made available by the Americans, made significant inroads into the Soviet systems.

Venona intelligence revealed the most extraordinary information. The Soviet Union had spies and informers embedded within the most secret American and British organisations, including MI5, MI6 and the Foreign Office; the National Security Agency (NSA) and even the Manhattan Project had been penetrated. With so many arms of the security services being compromised, the decrypts were restricted to the cryptanalysts and to a few select members of NSA and GCHQ; even President Truman and Prime Minister Atlee were denied access.

Mathematicians were able to demonstrate some success in decrypting Soviet traffic, but identifying the individuals involved was down to officers on the ground, from MI5 and MI6 and their American counterparts. Three individuals featured in the decrypts that came out of the mathematicians' work: *Homer*, later to be identified as Donald Maclean: *Mädchen* or *Hicks*, later to be identified as Guy Burgess: *Sonny* or *Stanley*, later to be identified as Kim Philby. All to be revealed in due course with *Johnson* or *Yan*, being Anthony Blunt: *Liszt*, being John Cairncross who had worked in Hut 3 at Bletchley Park.

> Cairncross was fearsomely intelligent, his difficult personality ensured
> that he was always being moved on. . . In 1941 he was moved to
> Bletchley Park, labouring in Hut Three on the Luftwaffe order of battle.
> His moment of triumph came in early 1943 when he was able to warn
> his KGB controller of the impending German armoured offensive at
> Kursk[43].

In 1948 tensions between the Western Allies and Russia began to accelerate towards a threat of open conflict. The Potsdam Agreement at the end of the war had divided the defeated Germany into four temporary occupation zones; the Russian zone completely surrounded Berlin which was, itself, divided into four zones within the Berlin perimeter. Since the end of the war the currency in circulation within Germany was, as had been during the Nazi regime, the Reichsmark, but inflation made that currency worthless and the new, American inspired, Deutschmark was introduced. Inflation in East Germany, which still used the Reichsmark, was out of control and so the Soviets introduced the Ostmark, but were concerned lest the Deutschmark should become the *de facto* currency in East Germany.

In order to prevent the Deutschmark spreading into their territory the Soviets blocked all road, rail and river access to Berlin. In retaliation, the Western Allies imposed similar blockades between Western Europe and East Germany; the Soviets cut off electricity supplies to Berlin from the generating stations within the territory that they controlled. With food running short the Berlin Airlift began, and the volume of intercepted Soviet wireless traffic increasing, the pressure on the mathematicians at GCHQ increased accordingly.

With the growing tensions between East and West, the Soviet-sponsored coup in Czechoslovakia resulted in a communist government on the very borders of those countries that were signatories to the Brussels Treaty of March 1948, just prior to the Berlin Airlift beginning. The growing crisis prompted the USA to initiate the formation of a new organisation, one which followed the ethos of the United Nations, but that could operate outside the UN Security Council, over which the Soviet Union could exercise a veto. Thus the North Atlantic Treaty Organisation (NATO) came into being in April 1949.

Meanwhile, the Berlin Blockade continued, with more and more flights and with a growing number of attempts at disruption. Upon signing the North Atlantic Treaty, the countries of Europe sheltered beneath the American 'nuclear umbrella' and GCHQ's intelligence gathering operations became further stretched requiring more and more staff, and more and more space in which to accommodate them. In May 1949, the Soviet Union finally lifted its blockade of West Berlin, although the Berlin Airlift continued for some months after, until the road and rail routes into the city were again fully open.

At GCHQ Eastcote, Hugh Alexander had been placed in overall charge of Section H, which was where Joan Clarke and her cryptanalyst colleagues worked. In many ways this was an arrangement with which Joan was very comfortable, being almost identical to that which had existed in Hut 8 at Bletchley Park during the war. Whatever temporary euphoria may have existed within Section H, it very soon evaporated; in late

August 1949 the West was taken completely by surprise when the Soviet Union conducted its first successful nuclear weapon test at the Semipalatinsk Test Site in Kazakhstan, three to four years before the security services on either side of the Atlantic had predicted.

The cryptanalysts at GCHQ Eastcote were galvanised into action to review much of the Soviet traffic which concerned Los Alamos, the American atomic bomb research establishment in new Mexico., home of the Manhattan Project under Robert Oppenheimer. The codename *Charles* was identified and was subsequently revealed to be Klaus Fuchs who, after interrogation by MI5 officer William Skardon, made a full admission in February 1950, finally being given a fourteen year prison sentence.

> *AUTHOR'S NOTE: Klaus Fuchs a German born theoretical physicist, was interned in the Isle of Man and then Canada at the beginning of the war but was released after two years. He worked on the British atomic bomb project and, immediately after the war, at the Atomic Energy Research Establishment, Harwell where he was arrested leading to a confession.*

Also revealed by further delving into references to *Charles* (Fuchs) it became apparent that the Soviets had made considerable efforts to gain information on jet-engine technology, giving them insight as to how atomic weapons might be effectively delivered. Also revealed was the presence of secret radio equipment in Oxfordshire operated by *Sonia*, in reality Ursula Beurton who left for Berlin before the Fuchs trial began. As with the wartime breaking of *Enigma*, it was vitally important to prevent the Soviet Union from becoming aware that their codes had been broken.

> But incredibly, the *Venona* secret itself was also compromised, in circumstances that were almost blackly comic. For among the very few who were invited in on the intelligence that these Soviet codes had been cracked were in fact two undercover Soviet agents. In the US, that agent was Elizabeth Bentley [codename *Gregory*]. For the British, it was the Cambridge spy Kim Philby[44].

The following year saw GCHQ Eastcote putting names to Soviet agents *Homer* (Donald Maclean) and *Mädchen* (Guy Burgess), but the security services were waiting before taking action. Donald Maclean's name was in circulation within the small circle of those entitled to know; one recipient of that information being Kim Philby in Washington who immediately dispatched Burgess back to London in order to warn Maclean of the imminent danger and advise him that he should immediately leave London for Moscow by an already formulated plan.

On 25th May 1951, late on a Friday evening, Guy Burgess and Donald Maclean went on board the SS *Falaise* for a weekend channel cruise, leaving from Southampton and landing briefly at St Malo, the French waiving the need of passports for such a short stop-over. At St Malo they disembarked but then made their way via Rennes, Paris, Berne and Zurich to finally reach Prague, safely behind the Iron Curtain of which Churchill had spoken in Fulton, Missouri.

Burgess and Maclean were already under suspicion by the Foreign Office and the fact of their disappearance was passed for investigation to MI6 who, searching Burgess's flat, found papers that compromised John Cairncross who, along with Burgess and Maclean, had been at Cambridge University during the pre-war years. Kim Philby was compromised but cleared of suspicion by the Foreign Office. However he was dismissed from his post in MI6 and left the security service for civilian life; working as a correspondent for *The Observer* and *The Economist*.

While the Burgess and Maclean defections were consuming valuable GCHQ resources, another crisis was developing on the Korean peninsular. Communist controlled North Korea invaded South Korea with the enthusiastic approval of China and the tacit approval of the Soviet Union, which expressed some reservations. China entered the world stage as another potential enemy for GCHQ to monitor, and whose wireless traffic had to be decrypted. The additional workload put further strains on the numbers employed at GCHQ Eastcote, and where to house them and the increasing amount of equipment required.

The War Office already owned two properties just outside Cheltenham in Gloucestershire; Benhill Farm and Oakley Farm, and it was this change of location that was earmarked for GCHQ's expansion. The two farms had been developed throughout the war by the addition of brick built blocks and a range of temporary huts, again similar to the evolution that took place at Bletchley Park, but this time for War Office use. When the move was first muted to employees at GCHQ Eastcote there was considerable resistance among the clerical grades, resenting the move from London to Gloucestershire, but key workers generally accepted the move.

Temporary buildings at GCHQ Oakley Farm, Cheltenham

(internet image)

The move was to begin in 1952 and be completed by the end of 1954. In 1952 Joan had married but she and her new husband John Murray, who also worked at GCHQ, were not to make that move, nor to remain in London, but instead to move to a small Scottish town; Crail in the county of Fife.

What Joan Murray was leaving behind was a GCHQ with a larger budget to fight the 'Cold War' and a new Director to succeed Edward Travis who had retired through ill health. Wing Commander Eric Jones was a veteran of Bletchley Park's Hut 3 and had proved himself as a liaison officer in Washington at the end of the war. Joan was leaving GCHQ as recruitment for additional staff for the move to Cheltenham was becoming something of a priority.

CHAPTER 11

ALAN TURING AND A PROPOSAL

When Joan Clarke first arrived at Bletchley railway station on Monday 17th June 1940, she had been aware that she was about to make a contribution to the war effort, but not exactly what that was to be, although she could not have doubted that she had been recruited for her skill and ability in the field of mathematics. She had been approached at the end of the previous year, by Gordon Welchman who had supervised her for geometry at Cambridge, but he had been prepared to wait for her to complete Part III of the Mathematical Tripos before she took up her post.

When she left Cambridge she returned, for a short time, to her parent's home at 193 Rosendale Road in Dulwich, spending time with them and with her sister Silvia, before taking up her new position. She was taking up her appointment as a civilian employee of the Foreign Office, although many of her friends had chosen to enlist in one of the armed forces. Joan was very much the academic type of person who could make a far greater contribution by freely using her brain in the national effort, rather than by simply following orders.

Joan had taken an early train from London, arriving at Bletchley and walking the short distance along Sherwood Drive from the railway station to the security fenced Bletchley Park, anonymous but clearly a War Office site as evidenced by the gatehouse and the military police in attendance. Joan had been sent a travel warrant, and a letter of invitation headed 'Room 47, Foreign Office' which she was required to show in order to gain entry. The details were checked against her 'identity card', which had been issued to her at the outbreak of war, and she was escorted to the reception building for the necessary formalities to begin.

Once inside the reception building she was interviewed and administrative matters attended to, not the least significant being her signing of the Official Secrets Act together with an explanation of what would be expected of her in that respect. Two provisions of the Act were the most significant for a civilian employee such as Joan, making it an offence to:

> Retain for any purpose prejudicial to the safety or interests of the State any official document, whether or not completed or issued for use, when he [she] has no right to retain it, or when it is contrary to his [her] duty to retain it, or fails to comply with any directions issued by any Government Department or any person authorised by such department with regard to the return or disposal thereof.

> Allow any other person to have possession of any official document issued for his [her] use alone, or communicates any secret official code word or pass word so issued, or, without lawful authority or excuse, has in his [her] possession any official document or secret official code word or pass word issued for the use of some person other than himself [herself], or on obtaining possession of any official document by finding or otherwise, neglects or fails to restore it to the person or authority by whom or for whose use it was issued, or to a police constable.

There was some temporary accommodation for staff to live within Bletchley Park but they were quickly helped to find accommodation within the surrounding area. Joan was found a billet, within cycling distance. Others were billeted further afield, with un-marked military transport provided for journeys to and from work. Many of the female staff recruited to Bletchley Park were from well-off families, the 'right' family background was considered to deliver a greater sense of responsibility and, as a consequence, acceptance of the need for security. The 'debutants', as they were known, could often afford to subsidise their meagre accommodation allowance with family money so that they could live in hotels and pay for taxi transport. Joan's promised wage was £2 per week although by the time she actually joined there had been a small cost-of-living increase.

As described earlier, Joan was to work with Alan Turing rather than with Gordon Welchman, but there was some comfort for a twenty-two year old girl, however well educated, to see the familiar face of her older brother's friend in that alien world of security under military rule. Joan's first full working day, having settled in to her billet on the Monday evening, was Tuesday proceeding to work for the following six days before taking the seventh off, which was her twenty-third birthday. For the first week Joan was set to work in the 'Big Room' before being transferred into the Seniors' Room with Alan Turing, Tony Kendrick and Peter Twinn.

Bletchley Park lake with mansion in the background

(author's photograph)

Joan's first impression of the atmosphere in the small cryptanalysts room was one of Turing, Kendrick and Twinn being on easy terms with one another. Turing's eccentricities were the subject of some humour amongst the others, they referring to Turing's cylindrical slide rule as his 'guessing-stick' and the 'girls' in the 'big room' teasing him about his age, suggesting twenty-one rather than twenty-eight; Joan said that she would put it even lower, 'schoolboy' even, if joking[45]. In fact, Alan Turing had retained much of his schoolboy terminology, including referring to a rubber eraser as a 'bungey'.

The men in the Seniors' room (Joan being considered an honorary man) were generally on first name terms, a departure from the school and university practice of using surnames only, one exception being Alan Turing who was generally referred to as 'Prof'; however, Tony Kendrick never managed to refer to Joan by any name other than Miss Clarke, he generally still preferring the simple 'Kendrick' of previous years. It was Kendrick that referred to her as becoming one of the 'sahibs', although that was a term which never entered into common usage.

The Seniors found that they needed to take time out to relax, away from the intensity of their work, and one of their favourite pastimes was to engage in 'schoolboy' games, including 'battleships' which Joan described in some detail, although unintelligible to someone who had no notion of the game.

> Battleships, for which one only needed squared paper and pencil – 10 x
> 10 squares, four squares in a row or column for your battleship, three
> for cruiser, two for destroyer, one for submarine: you fired ten shot
> virtually into chosen squares, the opponent reported how many hits
> there were, and each hit put one of your guns out of action[46].

At times the war came very close to Bletchley Park and, in common with the whole country, codebreakers were compelled to troop into the darkness of the underground shelter each time the air-raid siren sounded. It was during these periods of enforced idleness and informality that Joan and Alan Turing began to become better acquainted. One of Turing's idiosyncrasies while confined to the shelter was to knit pairs of gloves, but finishing off the fingers was beyond his ability and Joan's domestic talents were regularly brought to bear on that task.

> Some men, even if they did know how to knit, would have considered it
> infra dig to do so in front of their subordinates. Apart from finishing off
> the fingers of the gloves, I remember just one subject on which I knew
> more than Alan. He told me that his mother's last letter mentioned
> making 9lbs of jam from 4lb plums and 4lb of sugar – "but that's
> impossible, contradicting the Law of Conservation of Mass". I
> explained that for most jams, and particularly plum jam, one adds
> water[47].

The summer of 1941 was a time when Joan's personal interests were given an opportunity to develop. Her life had been spent in serious and intense study, immediately followed by the extreme intellectual challenge of Bletchley Park with men's lives at risk. She was just twenty-four years old, working as an equal with some of the best brains in the country, and watching the secrets of the Third Reich unfold before her eyes.

Joan Clarke and Alan Turing, working closely together on the naval *Enigma*, began to experience a growing personal friendship. Their work lives being dominated by a shift pattern did not make it easy to spend time together outside the work environment, however the Bletchley Park estate, with it's lake and sports-ground, made for pleasant strolls and informal picnics and most fine afternoons there were informal rounders games to join in with, or simply to watch from the side-lines.

Bletchley Park grounds

(author's photograph)

The two went occasionally to the cinema in Bletchley, or for a drink at one of the local pubs, and had a shared interest in chess, Joan matching him in intellect but not in experience of the game. Joan had been introduced to chess through attending Hugh Alexander's course for beginners, he being an 'International Master', and twice British chess champion. As a teacher, Alexander's credentials were unparalleled; winner of the British Chess Championship in 1938, represented England four times in the Chess Olympiads, and represented Cambridge University in the Varsity chess matches of 1929, 1930, 1931 and 1932. Like Turing he had been at King's College.

When their leave days coincided, or when Turing could engineer them to coincide, they would take time off together. Both owned, and were happy to ride, bicycles which gave them an opportunity to get out into the countryside and explore the natural world; Turing's interest being in the mathematics of nature, seeing the Fibonacci sequence in the leaf and petal arrangement of many common plants.

> *AUTHOR'S NOTE: A Fibonacci sequence is one in which the next number is the sum of the previous two numbers ie 1:1:2:3:5:8:13 etc. In nature the sequence usually shows itself wherever spirals occur; petals, leaf arrangements etc. The ratio between the numbers (1.618034) is frequently called the golden ratio or golden number, much favoured in Georgian architecture.*

It was not long into their friendship that Turing proposed marriage:

> I suppose the fact that I was a women made me different. We did do some things together, perhaps went to the cinema, and so on, but certainly it was a surprise to me when he said (I think his words probably were) "Would you consider marrying me?", but although it was a surprise, I really didn't hesitate in saying "Yes". And then he knelt by my chair and kissed me, though we didn't have very much physical contact. Now, next day, I suppose we went a bit of a walk together after lunch, he told me that he had this homosexual tendency, and naturally that worried me a bit because I did know that that was something which was almost certainly permanent. But we carried on[48].

Turing bought Joan an engagement ring, which she wore off duty but never at Bletchley Park, and they visited both the Turing and Clarke families. While in London a small engagement party was hosted at one of the Lyons Corner Houses by Joan's brother Martin[49]; otherwise, the engagement was kept secret from most of their colleagues. One exception to this general rule was Shaun Wylie, of whom Joan was fond, and he of her, working together long after the war was over.

At the end of August they took their permitted one weeks leave together, travelling by train from Bletchley to Portmadog in North Wales, they had with them bicycles and rucksacks. They spent their holiday walking in the mountains, although they suffered the consequences of not having had the foresight to obtain temporary ration cards. During their week's holiday Turing came to realise that the course they were following could not be sustained and, being an honorable man, could not, and would not, deceive Joan any further. In telling her of his decision Turing quoted the closing lines to Oscar Wilde's Ballad of Reading Gaol.

> Yet each man kills the thing he loves . . . the coward does it with a kiss,
> the brave man with a sword.

On returning to Bletchley Park they both continued their work as before. Alan Turing, ever the gentleman, made efforts to avoid them spending more time than necessary together at work, while ensuring that Joan did not see the end of their engagement as a rejection of her, but as a caring response to his dilemma. Despite the breaking off of their engagement there was no animosity and the two continued to be affectionate friends.

In November 1942 Alan Turing was sent to Washington with the British Joint Staff Mission with the aim of improving relations between the two countries. He and Joan were still spending time together outside of work and his farewells included a light-hearted comment that "the first thing I shall do is to buy a Hershey Bar"[50.]

> AUTHOR'S NOTE: The Hershey Bar was a popular American milk chocolate bar made by the Hershey Company and advertised as 'The Great American Chocolate Bar'. The brand would have been known to Joan and Alan, through contact with American servicemen who would have purchased the chocolate in the PX stores.

At the end of March 1943, Alan Turing finally returned to Bletchley Park from his trip from America, spending time with Joan in his room at the Crown Inn at Shenley Brook End,, where he hinted to her that they might consider renewing their relationship which had been terminated a little more than a year previously[51]. Whether the hint was too subtle, or whether Joan was simply too wise to allow her resolve to weaken, nothing came of their reunion except that the two friends again enjoyed one another's company.

While in Washington Turing had concentrated on possible developments in the field of secure speech scrambling and when he returned to England his efforts were concentrated in that area. Towards the end of the year he transferred to Hanslope Park, about ten miles north of Bletchley Park, an establishment with a distinct military flavour which did not sit comfortably with Turing's characteristic chaotic approach to work.

As the war came to an end Alan Turing and Joan Clarke worked together again, if only for a time. He returned to Bletchley Park to join her and others in tidying up, or more accurately destroying, all papers and documentation relating to *Enigma* and the extent to which it had been cracked by Bletchley Park. He spoke to Joan eagerly of the future of computing, as he had spoken to her previously of the concept of his 'universal' machine. He left to work at the National Physical Laboratory, she to transfer to GS&CS at Eastcote; and so their two lives continued separately.

Alan Turing lived in the London Borough of Richmond upon Thames during 1947, before leaving the National Physical Laboratory (NPL) and returning to Cambridge for a sabbatical period and then later moving to work in Manchester. There was a strong, but platonic, bond between the two Bletchley Park colleagues who continued to occasionally meet and sometimes write to one another.

In early March 1952 Joan Clarke received a letter that she had probably feared, although may have expected would come to her one day. Alan Turing's letter came from his home at 43 Adlington Road, Wilmslow just south of Manchester. He wrote to say that he had recently appeared at the local magistrates' court and had been committed to appear at the next Quarter Sessions, charged with gross indecency with Arnold Murray, a nineteen year-old unemployed man. Arnold had been remanded in custody until trial, Turing had been released upon £50 bail.

Alan Turing had also written to his brother John, explaining that he intended to plead guilty to the charge. John Turing appeared to have no idea that his brother was homosexual, and seemed to have little sympathy for his position. John Turing was concerned about his own reputation and persuaded his brother to plead guilty, so limiting the possibility of the public scandal reaching London and doing any damage to the family reputation. Being on bail allowed Turing to visit his mother in Guildford, she being quite supportive of his plight.

The general gist of the letters that Turing wrote to his friends and ex-colleagues was that he felt rather foolish having got involved with a young man who had then gone on to encouraging his friends to burgle Turing's house and then to involve the police, opening himself to prosecution as a consequence of his naïve statement. In his letter to Joan he confessed to her that there was a physical element to his homosexuality as well as an emotional one. He said of the police that they were not as savage as they used to be, comparing his present situation to that of Oscar Wilde at the end of the nineteenth century.

Joan's past relationship with Alan Turing had not been widely known at Bletchley Park, but among those who had transferred to Eastcote it was no secret. By the spring of 1952 she was already engaged to Jock Murray (no relation to Arnold Murray), a Lieutenant Colonel, retired from the army, and a new recruit to GCHQ Eastcote as a fluent Russian speaker. It was not in Joan's nature to have kept her past romantic relationship with Alan Turing, or their on-going friendship, secret and it is an indication of Jock's good nature and maturity that it did not cause any problem in their relationship. They were due to be married that summer and her support was offered without reservation.

Both men were found guilty at the trial on 31st March 1952 before Mr J Fraser Harrison, the judge; Arnold Murray was bound over to be of good behavior for twelve months, despite another outstanding offence to which he pleaded guilty; Alan Turing was placed on probation for twelve months on the condition that he "submit for treatment by a duly qualified medical practitioner at Manchester Royal Infirmary". The treatment was a one-year course of *stilboestrol*, a hormone that rendered him impotent and induced significant breast enlargement with associated psychological problems.

News of the conviction, and the removal of Turing's security clearance, reached Eastcote and the ears of his previous colleagues; even in a climate of secrecy, gossip recognises few boundaries. The news of Alan Turing's conviction, and the severity of the punishment to be exacted upon him, came as a shock to his friends and to those who knew him well. To many others, the news of Turing's homosexuality was a surprise and, at a time when homosexual practices between men were still a criminal act, not viewed by most with any sympathy or understanding. The public revelation that Guy Burgess, also a Cambridge man, was homosexual only served to fuel the fires of contempt.

Joan's life in Scotland, now married to Jock Murray, was interrupted by news that Alan Turing had died on the 7th June 1954. The circumstances were unusual, a post-mortem examination revealed that he had died from cyanide poisoning, but the inquest did not produce any evidence as to how the poison was administered. Instead it returned a verdict of suicide based on an assumption that Turing had deliberately consumed the fatal dose via an apple, found half eaten at his bedside. There was no explanation as to why tests were not carried out on the suspected source of the poison. Turing's homosexuality made him a security risk in the culture of the day, but if Joan had any suspicions about the security services she made no comment.

A chapter of Joan's life, previously closed, was now finally ended.

CHAPTER 12

CRAIL AND THE COLD WAR

In 1952 GCHQ was preparing to move to Oakley, near Cheltenham, and for Eastcote staff to be transferred to the new site. Joan Clarke had a major decision to make about whether she would transfer to Cheltenham or not. Joan was now engaged to be married to Lieutenant-Colonel John Kenneth Ronald Murray, who also worked at Eastcote and was preparing for transfer. John Murray was not a well man, and the two had to decide whether to set up their marital home in Cheltenham or whether John would benefit from retiring to enjoy a quieter life. Joan was thirty-six years old, had earned a considerable reputation within GCHQ, and could expect significant advancement in Cheltenham; John, although only forty-two, had already completed a career in the army before transferring to Eastcote, but could not be considered a 'high-flyer' within GCHQ.

Joan and Jock's marriage at Chichester Cathedral. The small girl is Christine Clarke, Joan's niece and god-daughter.

(courtesy of John Clarke, Joan's nephew)

Joan Clarke married Jock Murray, who gave his home address as Ruislip in Middlesex, on Saturday 26th July 1952 at Chichester Cathedral. She left her parent's cottage in Vicar's Close, walking with her father through the cloisters and into the aisle where the congregation was made up almost entirely of their two families; friends and work colleagues were noticeably absent in consequence of the secret world which both the bride and groom inhabited. The marriage ceremony was performed by the Right Reverend, Bishop of Chichester, George Bell who signed himself 'George Cicestr', in the traditional style, and was witnessed by Jock's father Kenneth, Joan's brother Basil, Jock's married sister Heather Cocks, and Joan's cousin, Denis Clarke.

> The wedding took place at Chichester Cathedral on Saturday Miss Joan Elisabeth Lowther Clarke MBE MA, youngest daughter of Canon and Mrs W K Lowther Clarke of 4 Vicar's Close, Chichester, and Lt-Col John Kenneth Roland Murray, only son of Mr K G V Murray of the Egyptian Government (retired) and the late Mrs Murray of Cuckfield, Sussex. The bride and bridegroom met in the Foreign Office at which both were officials. Miss Lowther Clarke had twelve years' service and Lt-Col Murray, who joined the Foreign Office after leaving the Indian Army, is retiring shortly after six years. They are to live at his home, Priors Croft, [14 Nethergate] Crail, Fife, Scotland.

> Given away by her father, who was Canon in residence at the Cathedral, the bride wore a day-length dress of duck-egg blue and carried a bouquet of pink and mixed carnations. In attendance was her five-year-old niece, Christine Clarke, wearing a pink dress and carrying a Victorian posy.

> The ceremony was conducted by the Bishop of Chichester [Dr G K A Bell] assisted by the Rev C H Sinclair. Best man was the bridegroom's friend and war-time colleague, Mr Arthur Walsh. Mr H A Hawkins was at the organ. Later a reception was held at the bridegroom's home[52].

Joan's father, William Kemp Lowther Clarke, was one of the canons at Chichester Cathedral, which enabled him to arrange for the marriage of his daughter to take place at the cathedral. His connection with Chichester Cathedral had begun in 1943, when he was invited to join the Cathedral Chapter as the Bursalis Prebendary, an appointment usually made in recognition of theological gifts. Two years later he became a full Residentiary Canon, he and his wife Dorothy moving to Vicar's Close, which meant taking a full part in the life and worship of the Cathedral. In addition he served as Cathedral Communar, with financial and broader maintenance responsibilities; for a time he was also Cathedral Librarian. The cottage was, in fact, a large four bedroomed house, spacious enough for their family to visit and stay quite comfortably.

William Clarke's time at Chichester Cathedral had not been entirely without controversy. In 1947 he had found himself embroiled in a bibliographical scandal[53] when he decided that the Cathedral Library contained a number of antiquarian books that were never consulted and, with very little space available, were standing in piles on the floor. Many of these books pre-dated the death of Henry VIII, some were thought to have been owned by the king himself, including a copy of *Vilagut,* which had some considerable value. William, as librarian and communar, made the decision to sell these books through Sotheby's via their November sale.

Bishop Bell was very unhappy with the decision to sell the books and complained bitterly that William had overstepped his authority. There were acrimonious discussions within the cathedral but it was finally established that the contents of the library were, in fact, the property of the Dean and Chapter, over which the Bishop did not have authority. William, as librarian and communar, required only permission of the Dean and Chapter to manage and dispose of the cathedral's assets as and when necessary. As a compromise William journeyed to London and bought back the copy of *Vilagut* for the cathedral, Sotheby's having already found a private buyer.

There seems to have been no further friction between the Bishop and the Communar except Bishop Bell's later writings criticising the holding of both posts by a single person; warning of a possible conflict of interest between the Librarian, who seeks to buy or sell, and the Communar who authorises such actions. Having come to an understanding on that matter, life at the Cathedral seems to have continued quite uneventfully. William was an academic at heart and, prior to his appointment at

Chichester, had spent a number of years as Editorial Secretary of the Society for Promoting Christian Knowledge (SPCK) and his leanings towards the study of books, publishing and library collections fitted him very well for his cathedral role.

Jock Murray had been a career soldier. Born 1910 he attended Wellington School from the age of fourteen and then the Royal Military Academy, Sandhurst, being commissioned in September 1930. His father worked for the Egyptian government and, although a Scot, made the family home in Cheltenham where Jock (John Kenneth Ronald) Murray was born. On leaving Sandhurst he left immediately for India. His first placement was with the 2nd Battalion, Duke of Wellington's Regiment. After one year he was transferred to the 2nd Battalion, 4th Bombay Grenadiers (later renamed the Indian Grenadiers), where he served as a regimental officer in Ahmednagar, Manzai, Wana, and Rawalpindi. His later years of service were spent in military intelligence.

In 1937 Jock was sent to the School of Slavonic and East European Studies (SSEES) in London. During the run-up to war, the Intelligence services were active in preparations to combat the anticipated threat from Stalin as well as from Hitler and, whereas German was quite a widely known language, few people were familiar with Russian. The formal tuition complete, successful students were then sent to one of the Baltic states to live with a Russian speaking family and to experience full immersion, living with the language and isolation from English conversation. By the end of 1938 Jock had qualified as an interpreter, returning to India by the time that hostilities began.

During the war Jock was based in Delhi at the Wireless Experimental Centre (WEC), one of two overseas outposts of GC&CS, the other being the Far East Combined Bureau, which concentrated on breaking Japanese codes. The WEC was located several miles outside the city and hence secure, being staffed from the Intelligence Corps, the British and Indian armies and the Royal Air Force. After the war he was seconded to the War Office in London, and retired from the Army 1948, with an annual pension of £480. Then, with his Russian knowledge, Jock was offered a position with GCHQ at Eastcote where he met Joan Clarke. His address at that time was in Cumberland Mansions in the centre of London although by the time of his marriage he had settled in Ruislip, much closer to Eastcote.

AUTHOR'S NOTE: Alan Stripp also spent time at WEC Delhi, as a contemporary of Jock Murray. There he intercepted, deciphered and translated Japanese wireless traffic.

Crail in Fife was a rather curious choice of location for Mr and Mrs Murray to buy a house and settle down. Joan had no family connection with the village, or with Fife, or even with Scotland. Although descended from a Scottish family, Jock's closest connection with Scotland was through his grandparents, originally from Aberdeen but who lived most of their lives in England.

Joan and Jock's home in Nethergate, Crail

(author's photograph)

Crail was a small fishing community on the Firth of Forth with a sheltered harbour. Fishing offered a living to some but generally it was a wealthy community. Some worked on the golf courses; Crail had its own course but Royal St Andrews was not too far distant. What Crail did not offer was a hospital, and considering Jock's poor health this seems a strange choice unless any of the military facilities in the area could be called upon.

Just outside Crail lay HMS Jackdaw, a naval airfield, which had operated as a torpedo attack training school during the war, but was closed in 1947, although not abandoned. The airfield was used by The Black Watch at various times in the 1950s, acting as a staging post for them on their way to Korea, but was earmarked for a role during the 'cold war', an interest that was to dominate the attention of the security services during the following years. The airfield's role was not entirely clear and was the subject of speculation by the Soviet Union, which dispatched Guy Burgess to investigate the site in the year before his defection to Moscow.

About five miles away from the airfield, RAF Troywood was originally built as a radar station during the war but was completely rebuilt as part of the ROTOR early warning system in 1951. The guardhouse was built to resemble a farmhouse, but reinforced with concrete and steel girders, leading by way of a one hundred and fifty metre tunnel to an underground bunker intended as a regional command centre should Britain suffer nuclear attack. The facility, renamed RAF Anstruther, was in continual use as a cold war radar station. A little further distant from Crail Airfield was the Hawklaw Y Station, still being used in 1952 as a GCHQ controlled Y station, masquerading as a long distance radio station, which continued to intercept messages, primarily from the Eastern Block throughout the 1950s.

In 1952, Jock Murray was in his early forties. Joan Murray (Clarke) was only thirty-six years old and considered a vital part of the code breaking section (Section H) within GCHQ; her mathematical and technical abilities having been proven during the war years. Jock Murray, an experienced soldier and intelligence officer with an excellent knowledge of Russian, was the epitome of the personnel that GCHQ needed during the cold war. In view of the fact that together they were too valuable an asset to let simply disappear, to be replaced by trainees, perhaps the choice of Crail to set up home might be more readily understood.

By coincidence perhaps, the Joint Services School for Linguists (JSSL), founded in 1951, planned to consolidate its operations at Crail airfield, its other schools at Bodmin in Cornwall and Coulsdon, near Croydon eventually closing. There is a strong possibility that Crail airfield, secure and strongly guarded, was also the site of other activities; perhaps a spy school, as the Soviets thought, perhaps an ultra-secret GCHQ listening and analysis centre; perhaps an MI5 counter-intelligence facility.

Crail's two newest residents had chosen, by chance, to live in in the centre of a cluster of 'cold war' military establishments. They lived quietly in Nethergate, following their hobbies, Jock even writing a history of the town, until at Christmas 1961, he decided to write a letter to an old friend. Wilfred Bodsworth was still working at GCHQ in Cheltenham but who lived in Guiting Power, a small village in the Cotswolds. The letter was from one old friend to another. The two men had met at Eastcote, although Joan had known 'Boddy' at Bletchley Park during the war years. Jock wrote that he was quite well again, after the illness which had prompted his 'retirement' from Eastcote, and generally reported that he and Joan were both in good health. Bodsworth immediately showed Jock's letter to Hugh Alexander, who then quickly wrote back:

> Boddy showed me your letter from which I am very pleased to see that you are now a great deal better in health – and it is this that prompts this letter. Is there any chance (question expecting the answer no but hoping for yes) that you and Joan would like to come back here if only for a few years? If there were I would see whether we could get round staff side difficulties (I think there is a good chance that we could) and make you a decent offer. You would both be very valuable to us – there is a lot to do on Boddy's side and he would be delighted to have you back and Shaun Wylie is equally enthusiastic about having Joan.

> Work here I would say is generally more varied and interesting in 'H' than when you both left. I very much hope that – unless health considerations rule it out – you will consider this seriously. The 'staff side' problem mentioned above is the difficulty of bringing people in anywhere except at the bottom of the ladder; I think however that the argument on the basis of special qualifications would be so strong in your case that we should be able to manage it.

> Best wishes to you both; Shaun who brightened visibly at the possibility of Joan's return – sends the same.

Wilfred Bodsworth replied to Jock's letter directly assuring him and Joan of a warm reception if they were to visit Cheltenham, inviting them to stay with him and his wife, Sally, and offering to lend them a car for the duration of their stay, although Jock and Joan did have a car of their own.

When Jock and Joan Murray replied to Hugh Alexander's letter they showed no sign that they may have had any such return to Cheltenham in mind, professing that they were well settled in Crail but, on consideration, they were warming to the idea. However, they did question whether their 'very rusty' qualifications would be of sufficient value, given their time away, and suggested a trial six month contract to begin with.

In the initial draft of this letter, Jock and Joan had originally included the phrase "We feel it only right that we should come in somewhere near to the bottom of the ladder" but this was removed from the letter which was sent to Hugh Alexander. The draft also makes mention of "a host of problems to be solved here in Crail, needing careful thought before we can come to any decision" but this, again, was omitted from the final version.

Jock and Joan did actually visit GCHQ Cheltenham in the middle of February, the delay being the result of the Security Division insisting upon further vetting of Jock, covering his years in Scotland. The visit to Cheltenham resulted in them both receiving offers to return to GCHQ, Jock being offered a temporary position, with no pension, starting 19th March and an offer of help finding accommodation for him and Joan while they organised their relocation. Jock's probationary period was completed by the end of July and his position was then made permanent, and a salary of £1,295 pa confirmed.

Given the duplicitous nature of the security services, the question of why Jock's letter to Wilfred Bodsworth had the immediate effect of eliciting an offer of returning to GCHQ, just as activities in Crail were winding down, and at a time when Jock and Joan would be prepared to consider such a move possible, remains unanswered. From the correspondence it seems as though Joan had never retired from GCHQ, no vetting, no probationary period and an appointment going straight back in to work with her former colleagues in Section H.

If any clues to subterfuge were to be found they would lay in Wilfred Bodsworth's reply to Jock's letter. Boddy, writing in longhand, from his home address in Guiting Power, about thirteen miles outside Cheltenham.

By the time this reaches you, you will have realised that your letter has had repercussions here. Hugh Alexander discussed it with me and made his offer immediately. I don't expect for a moment that you will accept it, but would be very pleased if you did. Since you left there has been no one quite like you on what you did and there is now more than ever to do.

Our village is much like yours in many ways. A small group of retired folk (women) is active and women's organisations flourish. But the aboriginals predominate on the whole and a further difference is that we have a squire (a new one) who has given the whole place a face-lift. When this is finished the place will rank among the Cotswolds as having 'character', without the risk of its being exploited commercially as some others are nowadays[54].

Interestingly there is no mention of Joan, yet it was she and Boddy that worked together at Bletchley Park, and Joan's mathematical abilities would be of greater value to GCHQ than would Jock's language skills; however, Boddy was a language specialist, rather than a mathematician and, working on the Venona project, might have considered that more significant. It is Hugh Alexander's letter that mentions Joan's return to GCHQ and identifies his own section, cryptanalysis, as being more interesting than previously. The letter could easily be interpreted as Joan returning; Jock as being re-employed. The second paragraph of Wilfred Bodsworth's letter also implies that there had been some contact between Jock and Boddy in the intervening years, Boddy clearly knowing something of Crail, perhaps a visit; perhaps Jock and Joan visiting Cheltenham.

Many years later, Shaun Wylie placed Joan at GCHQ Cheltenham in 1958, perhaps visiting friends, perhaps for work. If Joan had continued with some role during her years in Crail it would be quite reasonable for her to have made occasional visits to GCHQ. If Joan was not working for GCHQ in 1958 then Wylie could not have seen her at Cheltenham; but Wylie had known Joan since the war years, a close enough friend to have been made privy to her and Turing's engagement, and it's unlikely that he would have made an error in identifying her.

CHAPTER 13

MEDALS AND NUMISMATICS

When Jock Murray retired from the army in 1948 to settle at Cumberland Mansions in London, he began to take an interest in medals and medal ribbons. He had been in the British army, and the Indian army, for eighteen years and made a great number of friends in India, with whose help he assembled a collection drawn primarily from the Indian princely states. Added to these was a small collection of English milled gold coins, sufficient to justify his joining the Orders and Medals Research Society (OMRS), which began regular meetings at the War Museum in London. At about the time that he and Joan were married, and preparing to move to Scotland, Jock sold his collection through the London auction house of Glendining & Co.

> *AUTHOR'S NOTE: Indian Princely States refers to semi-sovereign principalities in the Indian subcontinent during the British Raj. At the time of the British withdrawal in 1947, over five hundred and sixty princely states were officially recognised before effectively ceasing to exist with India's independence.*

Once settled in Crail the couple began to take an interest in their immediate surroundings such that Jock was inspired to delve more deeply into the history and architecture of the parish. Jock trawled the Burgh records held in the Town Hall and, as a result of his interest, was appointed the Burgh Archivist, giving him unrestricted access to the necessary records. His research took him to Edinburgh and, nearer to home, involved reading through four thousand back numbers of the *East Fife Observer* and the *East of Fife Record*. His typewritten notes were completed in 1960, not published in any conventional sense, but lodged with the parish archive, for the benefit of future historians.

> *AUTHOR'S NOTE: Crail airfield is clustered into two groups of buildings, the western group consists of the non-operational sector (barrack blocks, church and cinema) and the eastern group being the operational sector (control tower, hangar, dispersal bays, runways, engine and aircraft armament repair shops). Crail is one of the best*

preserved Second World War airfields in Britain and the whole site has been listed.

Jock made scant mention of Crail airfield in his notes although, given his and Joan's position and knowledge, this may have been quite deliberate.

It was first the base of No.527 squadron, a unit that distinguished itself in the attack on the German battleship *Tirpitz*. Later, as HMS Jackdaw, it was developed as a Naval Air Torpedo School for training Barracuda pilots for the Fleet Air Arm. It was raided three times by German aircraft in 1941-42 . . . taken over by the War Office for the Joint Services School for Linguists.

On 13th May 1952 HM Elizabeth the Queen Mother, as Colonel-in-Chief of The Black Watch, inspected and bade farewell to the 1st Battalion of that regiment at the RN Air Station before its departure for Korea. On 21st September 1954 the Queen Mother again visited the RNAS and inspected the 2nd Battalion of The Black Watch prior to its dispatch to British Guiana[55].

Jock's notes spanned the entire period from Roman occupation through to 1960, covering the industries, the people, and their lives. Crail had the benefit of charters and liberties granted by Robert the Bruce, through to Queen Mary and Charles I in 1653. Trade with the Baltic States brought prosperity; the collapse of the fishing industry prompted decline. The Church's actions against fornication, adultery, loose women in general, and breaking the Sabbath were detailed, as were the persecution of witches including their burning.

Crail was witness to the Jacobite rebellions of 1715 and 1745, also the development of the three hundred and fifty year old Sauchope golf course and its decline after the construction of the new Balcomie course with its Balcomie Links Hotel. He mentioned the Town Hall with its distinctive Dutch tower and the restored Market Cross, the castle and the priory, the schools, the railway station and the harbour.

Jock's work as Burgh Archivist, and the writing of his notes, seems to have occupied whatever time he had available to him in Crail. There is no suggestion within Jock's notes, which were published in 2010, to suggest that Joan was in any way involved. While Jock was busy on his academic project, Joan appears to have made the overnight transition from her security work as a mathematician and codebreaker to being simply a housewife in a small isolated parish.

On their return to England, and to their new home at 13 Homecroft Drive in Uckington just outside Cheltenham, there was a short pause to Jock's studies, in both the historical and numismatics research. However, within a year he had resumed his interests in coins and had become a member of the Cheltenham Numismatic Society, adding to the small number of coins which he had retained from his previous collection. Within a year his interests began to be centred on Scottish coins, based around a Scottish 60 shilling piece of Charles I by Nicholas Briot, a French émigré, appointed chief engraver to the Royal Mint.

Scottish 60 shilling piece of Charles I

(internet image)

Jock's enthusiasm for numismatics encouraged Joan's interest and in 1965 she joined the British Numismatic Society. Jock joined the Royal Numismatic Society, writing articles for Spink's Numismatic Circular in 1966 and 1967 and then a piece for the Royal Numismatic Society's Journal in 1968, on *The Coinage of Mary Queen of Scots in 1553*. His research was thorough and accurate, as demonstrated by his introduction to his paper.

The coinage of 1553 comprises gold forty-four and twenty-two shilling pieces, silver testoons and billon bawbees and half-bawbees. No Act of Parliament or of Privy Council has survived concerning the gold and silver issues. There are, however, two Acts of Privy Council, dated January 1553/4, which explain the circumstances why a coinage of bawbees was needed at that time. There are also brief references to this coinage in one of the Hopetown MSS entitled *Anent Cunyie ane ample discourss*. The Accounts of the Lord High Treasurer of Scotland for the year 1553 contain the following reference: "*Ultimo Maii Item, to ane boy send to my Lorde of Sanctandrois being in Paslay with letterris to proclame new cunze in Air and other borrowes of the west cuntre, and his wage*"[56].

The following year Jock, again, published in the Royal Numismatic Society's Journal; *The Silver Scottish Coinage of Charles II*, which appears to have involved a number of trips to Scotland for research purposes, both to Edinburgh and to Lauder Castle in the Borders. His attention to detail and meticulous research using unpublished material is typical of the man, and his acknowledgements of assistance are fulsome and genuine.

I am much indebted to Mr Ian Stewart for reading through an early draft of this paper and making many suggestions for its improvement; to Mr. R. B. K. Stevenson for lending me photographs of all Charles II silver coins in the National Museum of Antiquities, Edinburgh; to the Dowager Countess of Lauderdale for permission to search through the mint papers at Thirlestane Castle; and to the staff of the historical search room, Scottish Record Office, Edinburgh, for all the assistance I received during numerous visits there[57].

Jock had another piece published in Royal Numismatic Society's Journal in 1970; *The Scottish Gold and Silver Coinages of Charles I*, a comparative work to that of the previous year. By all accounts Jock was a kind and well-mannered man who attracted only a single complaint from others in the field of numismatics, which was "that he was too diffident about the value of his work to others". His gentle language is best exampled by:

> Burns' chapter on the coinage of Charles I in volume II unfortunately contains a number of uncorrected slips of the pen. In particular, the figure numbers given in the text do not always correspond with the coins they are said to illustrate. Burns died when only the first volume had passed through the press, so the remainder of the work lacked his careful supervision[58].

Joan's interest in numismatics had been growing during the early years of their return to GCHQ in Cheltenham and by 1971 she felt able to venture into print for the first time. Her subject was coinage from an earlier period than had been studied by Jock in his earlier pieces. The coinage of James III (1451-1488) who reigned from 1460-1488 and James IV (1473-1513) who reigned from 1488 to 1513, both of Scotland, demanded a very high degree of technical knowledge and analysis to write such a paper. The detail is very impressive, but her background knowledge of her subject is also very clear from her writing.

> Before going into detail about the coins struck in this period, it is desirable to fill in some of the background. Up to the middle of the sixteenth century the standards and types of the silver coinage of Scotland were influenced mainly by those of England. Although there were long periods when the weight standards were different, conformity with England was re-established in 1357 and 1451, as well as in 1484, and also proposed in 1366 and 1424. These weight standards, when laid down in terms of the Scottish Troy ounce, may actually have been slightly below those of England, since at the union of the crowns the Scottish mint ounce was found to be lighter than the English Troy one by nearly nine English grains. Presumably the same was true of the Scottish ounce in the fifteenth century, but certainly no account was taken of such a difference in quoting the standard weight in 1451: according to the Act of Parliament in that year, new money

'conformit evin in wecht to the mone of Inglande' was to be struck, at eight groats to the ounce, and to have the same currency value as 'the Inglis grote of the quhilk viij grottis haldis ane unce'[79].

In 1972 Jock, having finally retired from GCHQ, submitted a joint paper with Ian Stewart, later to become Baron Stewartby of Portmoak, which would become Jock's last paper for eight years. The subject was *The Scottish Copper Coinages, 1642-1697* and detailed the low value coins of the period, known as *billon bawbees*, debased coins having the value equivalent to an English half-penny. In the introduction the two authors are detailed as making specific contributions; 1642-1668 Jock Murray and 1691-1697 Ian Stewart; the intervening period being a joint work[60].

The following six years were somewhat fallow as regards publishing and then it was Joan's reduced work responsibilities that allowed her to devote more time to her numismatics studies, and to publish a contribution to the British Numismatic Journal, titled *Elvet Moor, Lumphanan and Drumnadrochit Finds of Late Fourteenth-Century Scottish Coins*. The subject had been thoroughly examined during the *Second Oxford Symposium on Coinage and Monetary History* the previous year, but Joan's studies enlarged on County Durham (Elvet Moor), Aberdeenshire (Lumphanan) and Inverness-shire (Drumnadrochit) on the west shore of Loch Ness.

In her contribution, she again demonstrated a deep analytical approach to her subject and she employed a deductive approach to determining the origins of the Elvet Moor hoard:

> It will be apparent that I do not think it likely that this pot hoard represents the cash of a traveller from Scotland, although not casting any doubt on that as an explanation for some of the smaller finds of Scottish coins beyond the borders of that country. The composition of Elvet Moor hoard is certainly exceptional for England, although Scottish coins were at this time allowed currency in England, and Neville's Cross hoard may be representative of the circulating medium in the area: in this, although English coins predominated, they were mainly pennies, whereas the Scottish were groats and half-groats and

gave nearly half the value, even reckoned at their English currency value of threepence (from 1373 to 1390). This valuation of the somewhat lighter Scottish coins would provide a reason for the owner to separate off the Scottish portion of his spare cash, if only for convenience in reckoning[61].

Similarly, when discussing the Lumphanan and Drumnadrochit hoards, Joan pointed out that the "few old coins" found when repairing the church-yard dykes were used to purchase mortcloths, otherwise funeral palls, for the parish poor.

The following year, 1979, Joan published again, this time concerning *The First Gold Coinage of Mary Queen of Scots*, when the mint was under the control of Sir William Hamilton of Sanquhar and his partners for one year and they were permitted to:

> . . . stryke and prent ane ducat of gold of the fynes of xxiii caractis fyne and of the wecht of thre penny wecht of the avale of xx s. money of the realme of Scotland; and als to stryke and prent ane croun of the sone of fynes of xxi caractis and ane half, nyne of thame makand the unce wecht, of the price of xxii s. the pece.

Writing for a knowledgeable audience, Joan did not include a translation from 'Old Scots'. She goes on to identify nineteenth century forgeries, which were struck from dyes cast from genuine coins, pointing out small differences from the effects of double striking. Her analytical skills, and attention to the smallest inconsistency, were entirely in keeping with her work at Bletchley, Eastcote and Oakley. She credited her husband "for most of the work on old catalogues, used here, as well as for very helpful discussion; and to the various museum authorities for access to their coins, provision of weights, and other assistance".

> *AUTHOR'S NOTE: Scots, contraction of Scottis, refers to the version of the Germanic language spoken in Lowland Scotland. Although English was widely spoken in Scotland it had arguably become a distinct language by the beginning of the fifteenth century.*

Away from work, Joan and Jock Murray wrote their 1980 contribution to British Numismatic Journal as a joint submission, *Notes on the Vicit Leo Testoons of Mary*

Queen of Scots. They made reference to both Jock and Joan having made contributions on this subject in previous submissions. These notes concentrated mainly upon the very small differences between the coins, so identifying the various 'mint masters' in office from time to time and which mints were operating, and where. A significant element of their work was an examination of Scottish history and of the English and French conflicts of the time. Jock had demonstrated, while living in Crail, his abilities in the field of historical research and his contributions are quite evident in the text.

> A brief survey of the history is necessary to put in context the known events directly affecting the Scottish mint in 1559 to 1560. By May 1559 Perth and Dundee had publicly adhered to the reformed faith. There was increasing militancy, both by the regent's government, which outlawed the protestant preachers, and by the 'congregation', which was joined by further prominent lords when the government garrisoned Perth. In June the insurgents had considerable success, and at the end of the month they entered Edinburgh, while the regent retreated to Dunbar. Before 1 July they 'stayed the irons' of the mint, an action which they claimed to be 'for most just causes', because of the quantity and baseness of the hardheads then being struck[62].

In 1982 Joan published, jointly with two others, another paper in the British Numismatic Journal titled *The Innerwick Hoard 1979*, in which she reports on workmen building the Torness Power Station, and their finding of a number of silver and gold coins in the ground-works. There was some suggestion of criticism that the coins were not immediately handed over to the National Museum in Edinburgh, and commented that "some had been inexpertly cleaned with vinegar, presumably by the finders". The paper included a long and comprehensive catalogue of the coins recovered and identified her co-authors as Dr Caldwell, of the National Museum of Antiquities of Scotland and Mrs Delme-Radcliffe, responsible for the identification and listing of the English coins present.

> This site was being cleared by machine for the erection of huts to house the men working on the nearby Torness power station project and

several coins were turned up by a bulldozer towards the end of June. A rumour to this effect reached the National Museum in Edinburgh and on the police being informed eleven coins were acquired from workmen on the site. Thanks to the help of the police and a campaign of publicity in the local press and radio the Museum was able to recover the rest of the coins from locals over the following few weeks. The one gold coin turned up on the site about a year after the initial discovery. Fifty-three of the coins were not found at Thurston Gardens itself but at the cement works at Dunbar where earth was taken from Thurston Gardens and dumped[63].

With Jock's health deteriorating, Joan's studies were abandoned in order to care for her husband. However, with his death in November 1986 she published for the last time in 1987, her final contribution to the British Numismatic Journal being a paper titled *The Coinage of the Marians in Edinburgh Castle in 1572*, in which she demonstrated a comprehensive knowledge of both her subject and of Scottish history.

The Marian coinage began in March 1572, according to the *Diurnal of Remarkable Occurrents*. This is one of two valuable unofficial sources of information about this coinage: it was written by a contemporary observer residing in Edinburgh, but has reached us through an ignorant and often careless transcriber[64].

While Jock's main interest was in Scottish coins, at one time he also collected coins of the Eastern Baltic States, up to the eighteenth century, an interest probably having its origins in the time he spent in that region at the end of his Russian language course. In 1977 Jock presented the collection to the Ashmolean Museum in Oxford; his Scottish coin collection was sold at auction after his death, similarly Joan's collection after her death.

In 1986 Joan Murray was awarded the John Sanford Saltus Gold Medal, the premier distinction of the British Numismatic Society, awarded triennially, on the vote of its members, for scholarly contributions to British numismatics.

AUTHOR'S NOTE: *The John Sanford Saltus Medal is the premier distinction of the British Numismatic Society, awarded every three years, on the vote of Members, for the recipient's scholarly contributions to British Numismatics. The award was established by John Sanford, an American past-president of the society and first awarded in 1914. An interesting condition of the award was that recipients must not have canvassed for the award in any manner.*

When Joan died in 1996, her obituary was fulsome in it's praise for her work in the field of numismatics, praising her knowledge and her attention to detail; similar praise to that for Jock on his death ten years before. She was said to have taken great pains to respond to correspondents (including eminent historians as well as numismatists) who sought her advice, and that the society had been fortunate that someone of her formidable powers should have turned her attention to medieval numismatics, with such remarkable effect.

CHAPTER 14

CHELTENHAM AND OXFORD

Jock and Joan Murray, once they began working back at GCHQ, purchased a bungalow in Uckington, a small village on the western outskirts of Cheltenham; number 13 Homecroft Drive had been built on land originally managed by the Cheltenham Homecroft Association but had by then been entirely given over to residential housing. The land, originally used for smallholdings, meant that the gardens, two hundred feet, were very long even by the standards of the day.

> *AUTHOR'S NOTE: The Homecroft movement was a system of combining land cultivation with working class housing in the suburbs. The occupier would still work in a factory or similar but each home would come with two-thirds of an acre of land on which the family could raise vegetables and fruit. The Cheltenham site was used as a model of the Homecroft movement in a 1928 piece written for the Sociological Review, describing ten houses being set in two parallel rows, with plans to increase the number to twenty-five.*

In 1968 Joan and Jock drove from their home in Uckington to Blackman House in the precincts of Chichester Cathedral to attend the funeral of Joan's father who had died 8th April of that year. He and his wife Dorothy had moved from their home in Vicar's Close when William retired as Residentiary Canon in 1963, into Blackman House, another church property just around the corner in Canon Lane.

The family gathered around Dorothy to walk the short distance, past their previous home in Vicar's Close and into the cathedral, following the same route as Joan had walked sixteen years previously on her wedding day. The funeral service was led by Roger Plumpton Wilson, Bishop of Chichester, as was appropriate for a cleric of William's standing and years of service.

> Canon W K Lowther Clarke, former Prebendary and Canon Residentiary of Chichester Cathedral, whose funeral took place at the Cathedral last week, was an ecclesiastical scholar with a number of

authoritative literary works to his credit. From 1904 he was a fellow of Jesus College, Cambridge, and from 1915 to 1944 Editorial Secretary to the Society for the Propagation of Christian Knowledge. In 1959 he brought this experience to bear in writing his 'History of the S.P.C.K'.

He was the author of 'Liturgy and Worship' (1932) 'Almsgiving' (1936) "The Prayer Book of 1928 Reconsidered' (1943) and the 'Concise Bible Commentary' (1953). He was appointed Prebendary of Chichester Cathedral in 1943 and Canon Residentiary in 1945, holding both these appointments until his retirement in 1963[65].

Leaving the cathedral through the main doors, the family walked past the entrance to the Cathedral School Memorial Gardens which had been financed by a gift from William in 1947, and had been formally opened by Princess Marina, Duchess of Kent who had unveiled a plaque to mark the occasion. William died a wealthy man and left Dorothy well provided for; however Blackman House was held during his lifetime only, through dint of his position as Honorary Canon, and Dorothy was now faced with the prospect of moving out of church property. In fact Dorothy's health was failing and she moved from Chichester to a small care home near Maidenhead in Berkshire and died a year later in 1969.

Cathedral School Memorial Gardens

(author's photograph)

Joan, at the centre of Britain's attempts at combatting the threats of the Cold war, was privy to the secrets of the Kennedy assassination, the doubts about Lyndon B. Johnson,

China becoming the world's fifth nuclear power and the start of the Vietnam War. More reassuringly, she was also witness to the beginnings of the understanding on the non-proliferation of nuclear weapons. In Britain the Prime Minister, Edward Heath, expelled over one hundred Soviet officials from Great Britain; the intercepts that gave Heath the evidence he needed was certainly the product of Section 'H'.

Joan and Jock Murray led a secret life at GCHQ, living closer to the realities of the Cold War than did the rest of the population. Outside their work, they lived a home life similar to one that many others would have recognised. Their large garden was cultivated and cared for, mowing the lawn, cutting the hedges and cultivating the vegetable garden. Joan's particular interest was in the cultivation of soft fruit, a specialty in which she claimed some expert knowledge, based more on theory than on practice. According to her friend and next door neighbour, Derek Leppard, an encounter with Joan during the summer months would often involve a discussion on raspberries; theory and 'best practice'. Joan's other idiosyncrasy was her pleasure and satisfaction in using the Latin names for her plants, rather than the common names, wherever possible.

GCHQ Oakley, Cheltenham in 1962

(author's photograph)

Derek Leppard paints a very human picture of Joan, not of the mathematician, nor of the keeper of Cold War secrets, but of a lady who lived in the real world and who lived a real domestic life away from the constraints of national security. Although both she and Jock drove the family car, Joan also owned a moped, a bright red 'Garelli step through', suited to those who wore skirts or dresses; modesty guaranteed. The sight of Joan riding the four miles to and from work, a clean white helmet flanked by a pair of mirrors on stalks from the handlebars, created a lasting impression.

One small anecdote of their time in Uckington was quoted thus: "On the wall in the hall of their bungalow was mounted a short curved sword. This was mounted in such a position that as you opened the front door it could quite easily come to the right hand. I remarked about the weapon to Jock on one occasion. Apparently it came from the North West Frontier region. I think you have to draw your own conclusions about its position!"

Jock had achieved some improvements in his position within GCHQ being promoted to 'Department Specialist' in 1964 but by mid 1970, approaching his seventieth birthday, he asked Hugh Alexander to intervene on his behalf to allow him to reduce his employment to just three days each week. This was agreed, Jock would work only Wednesdays, Thursdays and Fridays each week, beginning 1st July albeit with no lunch hours and a rather reduced paid holiday entitlement.

On 9th November 1971 Jock received formal notification that his employment with GCHQ would be terminated at the end of the year with the benefit of a small gratuity payment. In reality, Jock's health was beginning to deteriorate and the letter of termination had been a joint decision between him and GCHQ, reflecting his own decision to finally completely retire from work.

Jock was finding it more and more difficult to cope with his breathing difficulties. Derek Leppard describes him as quiet but with an easy manner, belying his remote schoolmasterly appearance. Having no children Jock watched Derek's son Richard with some curiosity, observing that "he spends his time using only one wheel of his bicycle", referring to Richard's penchant for 'pulling wheelies'. Jock, slow walking and quiet talking, was a favourite of Twiggy, the next door cat, who would make a beeline for Jock whenever he set foot in the garden, and demand his attention. Not that Jock appeared too often, having spent years in India he shunned the outdoors in anything but the warmest weather.

Although the couple were quite comfortably off, Joan took the opportunity of topping up her Civil Service pension entitlement by three years in 1972 and a further five years in 1973 which, together with Jock's Civil Service pension and his army pension, would provide for a comfortable retirement when that time actually came for her.

Joan's progress within GCHQ reached a further stage in March 1975 when she received a letter informing her that she had been recommended for promotion to 'Principal' grade. In keeping with previous experience, Joan was the only woman on a list of twenty-two candidates and, not surprisingly, received her promotion two months later backdated to February of that year. As a simple comparison, the Civil Service rank of Principal is claimed to be equivalent to Colonel or Group Captain in the armed forces.

In July 1977 Joan Murray finally settled upon a retirement date of 31st August to retire from her position as 'Principal' within GCHQ, having reached her sixtieth birthday, and the mandatory age of retirement for Civil Service women. However, her services too valuable and her energy too great, true to form she opted to continue working as a 'clerical officer' in 'H' Division starting the following day. This was very much a regulatory, or grading, matter and her actual work continued as before. Financially this was quite beneficial as she then began drawing her Civil Service pension of a little over three thousand pounds per annum, plus a lump sum of over nine thousand six hundred pounds. Joan, however, had to complain to the Paymaster General's Office that her pension was not actually being paid; an error that was soon rectified, with apologies. Joan was a daunting opponent when it came to detail.

On the 27th January 1978, Joan's eldest brother Basil died, at the age of sixty-nine, at 220 Henley Road, Caversham, the home where he and his wife, Eileen had lived for some years. Basil Fulford Lowther Clarke had attended school in Leatherhead, and then went to St John's College, Durham, before going to theological college at Ripon College in Cuddesdon, south Oxfordshire, in an entirely rural environment. He later worked in parishes across the Oxford diocese.

His boyhood interest in church architecture had continued through his student years and into adulthood and, by the time he died, he had visited and catalogued an enormous collection of detailed notes, but only on churches that he had actually visited:

> His acute judgement, underpinned by meticulous research among published material and original sources, meant he was able to identify and record the architects of many churches and furnishings — information which cannot be found in any single place elsewhere. You can tell as you look at the books how his talent, skills, and knowledge improved over time. The first entries are just two or three lines, but the further you go, the more detailed they become. It's a snapshot - a moment in time - of those buildings almost one hundred years ago[66].

Joan decided to finally retire from GCHQ at the end of June 1982, at the age of sixty-five, five years after the normal retirement age for women. For whatever reason she agreed to continue working on an ad-hoc basis for a further two months, guaranteeing at least eighteen hours each week. The end of August saw her final departure from GCHQ and her formal acceptance of the continuing provisions of the Official Secrets Act that would apply to her in retirement:

> My attention has been drawn to the provisions of the Official Secrets Acts which are set out on the back of this document, and I am fully aware that serious consequences may follow any breach of these provisions. I understand (1) that the provisions of the Official Secrets Acts apply to me after my appointment has ceased; (2) that all the information which I have acquired or to which I have had access owing to my official position is information which is covered by Section 2 of the Official Secrets Act, 1911, as amended, and that the Official Secrets Acts apply to all such information which has not already been made public; (3) that the sections of the Official Secrets Acts set out on the back of this document cover material published in speech, lecture, radio or television broadcast or in the Press or in book form or otherwise and that I am liable to be prosecuted if either in the United Kingdom or

abroad I communicate, either orally or in writing, including publication in a speech, lecture, radio or television broadcast or in the Press or in book form or otherwise, to any unauthorised person any information acquired by me as a result of my appointment (save such as has already officiallly been made public) unless I have previously obtained the official sanction in writing of the Department by which I was appointed; (4) that to obtain such sanction, two copies of the manuscript of any article, book, play, film, speech or broadcast, intended for publication, which contains information which I have acquired or to which I have had access owing to my official position, or of any material otherwise to be published which contains information, should be submitted to the Head of Department.

I hereby declare that I have surrendered any sketch, plan, model, article, note or document (whether classified or not) made or acquired by me during the tenure of my appointment save such as I have written Department to retain.

A few days later Joan received a letter, through the GCHQ internal mail system, from Sir Brian Tovey, noting that she had completed twenty years of service with GCHQ, since re-joining in 1962, and making mention of her contribution in the 'H' field over many more years.

Jock Murray died 8 November 1986 and was cremated five days later at Cheltenham Crematorium, his ashes being scattered in the crematorium garden in a double plot, the other reserved for Joan's ashes when the time of her own death came. She obviously had no plans to move away from her home in Uckington, although she would eventually die in Headington, her ashes to be scattered there.

In March 1988 Joan, now widowed, received a letter from an Amanda Littleboy of Guildford, re-opening a subject which had long been dormant.

For the past year I have been organising a project which aims to have a commemorative plaque placed on the house once occupied by Alan

Turing in Guildford. The scheme, which was inspired by Hugh Whitmore's highly acclaimed play "Breaking the Code", has now reached its final stages and we are planning an unveiling ceremony, due to take place in the spring. I an particularly delighted that Derek Jacobi, who played the part of Alan so successfully in "Breaking the Code", has shown great interest in the scheme, and I am making arrangements for him to come to Guildford to unveil the plaque.

Joan's reply, apologising for not being able to attend the unveiling of the plaque gives the first indication that she had health problems of her own "In normal circumstances I should like to attend and I hope to have fully recuperated by then from a recent operation, but I am uncertain of the effects of the expected radiotherapy." In response to Miss Littleboy's enquiry about Alan Turing's speech problem, Joan was quite dismissive, describing this as 'hesitancy' and expressing the opinion that it appeared only "when he couldn't take refuge in silence".

Despite earlier indications that Joan would see out her days in Uckington, in 1991 she did move again; to 7 Larkfields, Headington Quarry, near Oxford. She had a niece living close by and this did offer some familial support in her remaining years.

Mrs. Murray remained at Uckington for five years after her husband's death, but in 1991 she moved to Headington, not far from one of her Clarke cousins. Another reason for moving was to be within reach of the Ashmolean Museum and the Bodleian Library in Oxford. Also, while still at Uckington, she had developed a condition which restricted the use of her right arm and shoulder, and a smaller house with a minuscule garden could reduce the effort of maintaining a household as she got older. For long periods she was in considerable pain, and the increasing difficulty of writing was the main reason why she was not able to bring much of her later work to a conclusion[67].

Three years later in 1994, Joan's sister Silvia died in Ontario and Joan, despite her seventy-five years made the journey to her funeral. Although having crossed the Atlantic a number of times for work, it had always been Silvia who had made the journey down from Ontario to Washington, or wherever Joan was with a delegation or attending a conference. Joan travelled to London Ontario where she finally meet her sister's Canadian friends[68].

> The late Joan Clarke's visits included a week spent at the time of Silvia's funeral in December 1994. The service was at St. John the Evangelist Anglican church. "She was just the opposite to Silvia," Jane Dale, a London friend of the artist, remembered this week. Joan was "a very, very friendly person but quiet". Silvia had been close to an American air officer and kept his photograph - without discussing whose image it was - through her life. London friends were among those who came to understand the photo's significance. Silvia Clarke wore a ring, a sign of love for the officer. She came to North America because of that love, but the officer's wife would not divorce him, Jane Dale said. "She never spoke about it," Dale said. "It was a war romance."

> She [Silvia] studied art in night classes at Beal secondary school. . . a member of the Western Art League and the Gallery Painting Group, Clarke [Silvia] was known for landscapes and painting of flowers. Twenty years ago, an exhibition honoured her at St. Paul's Cathedral. Clarke [Silvia] died on Nov. 29, 1994, after battling lung cancer[69].

Silvia Clarke had enjoyed an interesting life. During the war years she had worked for the BBC, ostensibly as a secretary but possibly in a job that had a function more closely connected with security. In Silvia's obituary, published in Canada, she is mentioned as having had some connections with MI5. Not too much credibility can be given to such a statement, with no evidence to support it, but Silvia did point out to her nephew, during one of her trips back to Britain to see Joan, a remote manor house where "she worked during the war". However Silvia's friend in Ontario, Pat Goodland, reports that Silvia was a BBC (radio) producer during the war, specialising in foreign language broadcasts, mentioning names like Herbert Lom and Rex Harrison.

Silvia made her last journey to Britain in the year of her death at the age of eighty-three, and Joan to Canada at the age of seventy-seven. Two remarkable women.

Joan and Silvia at a family christening in 1988
(courtesy of William Clarke, Joan's nephew)

CHAPTER 15

PUBLISHING THE SECRETS

In early December of 1977 Joan received a letter from Andrew Hodges explaining that he had been commissioned by publishers, Andre Deutsch, to write a biography of Alan Turing to which he would like Joan to contribute by sharing her memories of Turing. Being aware of her possible reluctance, given the somewhat unfortunate personal relationship between the two, Hodges described his approach to Joan as being on a "delicate matter" but thought it important that one should not give the false impression "that mathematics and cryptanalysis were entirely male preserves".

The secrecy, or lack of secrecy, concerning Bletchley Park had not been in doubt before the mid-seventies but in the previous few years the waters had become muddy. This was, perhaps, not too difficult for those who no longer worked for GCHQ to navigate but Joan, still with day-to-day access to secret information, needed to proceed very carefully indeed. Having sought advice from GCHQ she felt able to 'proceed with caution' and made arrangements to meet Hodges in Oxford early in the new year.

It's something of a compliment to Jock Murray that Joan felt able to assist Hodges with his project. Joan and Jock must have thought that that chapter of her life was fully and completely forgotten. When they married in 1952 Turing was not yet known outside the rarified world of mathematics and those experimenting with early forms of digital computers. The very existence of Bletchley Park and what had happened there was still a strictly kept secret. Few outside Joan and Jock's families and their immediate friends would have known of the engagement.

Even when Turing died in 1954 it was not a subject of discussion in the press, except that the publicity in the newspapers was because of his homosexuality, rather than because of the loss of a brilliant mind. Whatever Joan's role was in Scotland, her association with the dead man was kept very hidden from the media. Joan's very existence was virtually unknown, let alone her role at Bletchley Park.

Early in 1980 Joan had an opportunity to comment on a number of points raised by Andrew Hodges, as he had promised at their first meeting. Most were technical queries but she did have an opportunity to request that she be referred to in the book as Joan Clarke, rather than Joan Murray, and to make reference to Turing's 'bloody little book', which contained a table of figures for assessing the significance of certain statistics. Joan took pains to explain that 'bloody little book' was not a pejorative term but that it really was somewhat bloodstained.

> He developed independently some ides which I believe were original, although found in later publications. He probably never considered what he did here as real mathematics, to be written up as such. What mattered then was that it contributed to the work of GS&CS. . . The basis was, I suppose a compound Poisson distribution. He later explained verbally to Jack Good most of what he had done, and Good wrote up the theory, including (I think) a satisfactory explanation of a correction term, the permanent bonus, where Turing had forgotten how it had arisen[70].

Joan's lasting regard for Turing was evident from her comments about him finding that his title of 'Dr' was very useful to him in America, but him not using it in Britain; his efforts to manufacture a chess set for her during the summer of 1941, using coal to colour the black pieces; and his habit of using the phrase 'taking balls out of urns' rather than the term 'standard distribution'.

However, she was not blind to his shortcomings in the matter of teamwork and referred to his work for other groups at Bletchley Park as being of limited use, not through want of intellect but through want of a collegiate approach; she suggests he had a general mistrust of the work of others.

> After he left Hut 8 (or rather was still there physically but working on possible applications of similar ideas for other parts of GC&CS) I really don't know how far he made a valuable contribution. In one case where I did participate in what he was doing, and later had to explain it, I then got the impression that he had only worked along the same lines as

someone else earlier, which suggests inadequate consultation with
others involved – perhaps an unfortunate aspect of what was in other
ways a strength, that he would want to start from the fundamentals of
the problem. Newman says perhaps a defect of his qualities that he
found it hard to accept the work of others.[71]

Still concerned about the Official Secrets Act, she asked again, "May I
see anything which refers to the work at Bletchley, to ensure that I
haven't inadvertently said too much".

Andrew Hodges' book *Alan Turing: the Enigma* was published in 1983. One effect of
the book being published was that Joan found herself in correspondence with old
colleagues who had, themselves, been contacted by others from Bletchley Park, and
from other potential writers. Peter Twinn wrote to her to say that he was being
bombarded by letters from Harry Hinsley, Gordon Welchman and Dennis Babbage and
complained that with forty years distance from events, he simply could not remember
the answers to their questions. He speculated that the flood of letters had been triggered
by Welchman's book which he dubbed *How I Won the War Practically Single-handed*,
but had written reviews of the various books for publication, commenting to Joan that
"I'm getting a bit wearied by the subject". This was a view shared by Jock Murray who
was reported to have said "It's high time we all gave the subject a rest".

In 1985 Joan was asked to undertake some consultancy work with GCHQ to assist
Harry Hinsley on some aspects of the official history of *British Intelligence in the
Second World War*, especially the breaking of the naval *Enigma* code. Joan's work
continued into May 1986, when she was debriefed, and as a result of the changing
situation, had her travel restrictions for China and the Iron Curtain countries extended
to May 1990, a further four years. Joan's contribution appears to have been chiefly
correcting some of the errors made in earlier volumes that Hinsley, who was also
Master of St John's College, had allowed to slip through. Relief in GCHQ was palpable
from a letter addressed to Joan from Ruth Martin.

You may be aware that Volume III Pt 2 of the Official History finally
reached the publishers during the second week of April, and that we all

heaved a huge sigh of relief. There were no complications concerning
your *Enigma* appendix which is to be Appendix 30, the very last in the
volume. . . I would also like to thank you, on behalf of the Department,
for being prepared to put in so many hours' research and for producing
such a clear and thorough account of a difficult subject.

In September 1991 a letter arrived at Joan's new home in Headingly from Alan Stripp
explaining that he and Harry Hinsley, by now Sir Harry Hinsley, were putting together
the recollections of various people who had worked at Bletchley Park during the war
years. The intention was to publish them as a book, with each contributor describing
how they were recruited, what working conditions they had, but would also include the
technical and operational problems that they had encountered. They were looking for
about four thousand words from each contributor, stressing that it should be
understandable to the general reader, but adding that there would be need to remember
that some subjects needed to be handled with discretion although "most were now
freely discussed in books and articles".

Joan wrote her piece for *Codebreakers: The Inside Story of Bletchley Park* but it was
October of the following year before a publisher was found, The Oxford University
Press, with a planned publishing date of September 1993. Alan Stripp had to admit to
Joan, and other contributors, that the commercial aspects of the venture had not been as
successful as they had hoped.

When we laid our plans we had reason to hope that several publishers
would make rival bids. That did not happen, and we were lucky to find
a first-class publisher to take it on at all. That in turn has affected the
finances. The advance has covered only the editorial expenses (mainly
in typing, postage, telephone, some fax and, above all, photo-copying)
and leaves no balance for payments to contributors. But we will report
to you again if the book later earns royalties above that advance, and
meanwhile each contributor will receive a free copy of the book when it
comes out[72].

The actual date of publication was Thursday 26th August 1993 at a small reception at the Imperial War Museum in London, where wine and canapés were to be served to invited guests. The euphoria of publication over, recriminations began. By the beginning of October, Joan was already in some dispute with Jack Good over the frequency that the German naval *Enigma* wheel order changed, she admitting her error, but pointing out an error on his part, referring to work completed before Good's joining Bletchley Park and his reference to hexagraphs rather than trigraphs. Good's response was to claim a superior knowledge of *Tunny*.

Joan at the launch of 'Codebreakers' in 1993
(courtesy of John Clarke, Joan's nephew)

Alan Stripp became part of this conversation between Joan and Jack Good, who was then at the Virginia Polytechnic Institute and State University. He wrote to Joan at the end of October, following some exchanges between him and Jack Good.

> Well done, convincing Jack Good of his faux pas; but how can we put it
> right? Letters to and from there take ages, and so can he. I wonder if
> you and I can concoct a revision together which I can then try on him?
> It's a tribute to your patience and goodwill that I ask you to help in this
> rescue mission on someone else's behalf. OUP can neither alter the text

nor insert an extra errata slip (about 30 items now, alas) pro tem, so we have some time.

It is unfair, but a well-deserved compliment, to ask you to help me to attempt the rescue. . . did you know that the Observer/Waterstones listed us as No.5 in the ten hardback best-sellers for last week, behind Susan Hill, Iris Murdoch (to whom we gave an Hon D Litt this June), and Sue Townsend (to whom we didn't), but ahead of Alan Clark, Martin Amis, Dirk Bogarde and Dick Francis – what a crew.

Following the publication of Andrew Hodges' book, many people have written about Alan Turing and of others who made a contribution to Bletchley Park. The majority of books have been about *Enigma* in some manner or other and the contribution that individual men, not women, have made. Most have been based on the breaking of the three rotor *Enigma* as used by the German army and air force; virtually nothing on the breaking of the naval *Enigma*, certainly not on the breaking of the four rotor machine. The work of Joan Clarke is generally dwarfed by the reputation of Alan Turing.

Many of the books published have concentrated on the personal reminiscences of the people who worked at Bletchley Park, decoders rather than cryptanalysts. The social side of life was very important and Joan, being removed by the nature of her job, and by the reserved nature of her way of life, is hardly ever mentioned. Her claim to fame seems simply that she was once engaged to Alan Turing.

CHAPTER 16

THE END GAME

Joan Murray wrote to her nephew John Clarke on 7th August 1996 from her home at 7 Larkfields in Headington, where she had lived for the previous few years. Her mood was bright and uncomplaining, despite her obvious discomfort and struggle.

> . . . Not that I'm about to die, although naturally I didn't like to be told of another cancer. At the time I was perhaps mainly pleased to get a diagnosis to explain the trouble with my right hand. Radiotherapy cleared that up to some extent, particularly as regards the pain, but my hand is still semi-crippled. Writing and many other things are still a problem.
>
> I thought of you when visiting Little Kimble church, near Aylesbury. My recollection is that you were interested in churches with wall-paintings, when you and Leila stayed a few nights with us in Uckington (and she took details of some old church records, for her employer). Anyway, you probably know the fine display in that little church. Unfortunately they had apparently run out of the explanatory leaflets.
>
> I've had to have a bit more help in the garden than other years, but I can just mow my little lawn, when it grows, and do some dead-heading and the like. TV and reading fill up a lot of my time. I saw a bit more than I intended of EURO'96 football, which brought back memories of when Jock took me to watch East Fife live. As today is cool and dry, I think I'll have a go at the garden, and even transplant some seedlings, before posting this, which I can't claim to be urgent[73].

Joan Murray died at her home in Headington on 4th September 1996. She had been planning to visit her sister-in-law. When she failed to arrive there was some concern and, finally the police in Headington were contacted. A visit to her home in Larkfields found that she had died of a heart attack in her bedroom. With no history of heart problems, the Coroner ordered a post mortem examination but no inquest was necessary, the cause of death being simply stated as 'Ischemic Heart Disease'

Joan's funeral was held at Holy Trinity in Headington Quarry on the 23rd September 1996. The church, where Joan attended services during the last years of her life, was built of the stone after which Headington Quarry was named. Located in a small undulating, even hilly, suburb of Oxford, the churchyard offers a small island of tranquility. Among the stones and memorials gathered within the churchyard wall is a monument to C S Lewis (Clive Staples Lewis) the Belfast born writer and theologian, who was buried there thirty-three years previously.

Holy Trinity Church, Headington Quarry

(author's photograph)

Joan's body was to be cremated, as had been Jock's. The short committal service took place at the Oxford Crematorium, with only family present, her ashes later scattered beneath rose bushes in the twenty-two acres of surrounding gardens. The beautiful manicured surroundings providing a peaceful resting place for one who had known of, if not seen first hand, the suffering of two wars; a violent and confrontational World

War and a cruel oppressive and insidious Cold War; but in her last years to see the end of that war perhaps becoming a reality.

Memories of Joan came from both the world of numismatics, which was her hobby, and from that of cryptology, which had been her life's work. In numismatics it was generally considered that her greatest achievement was to establish the sequence of the gold unicorns and heavy groats of James III and James IV, an extremely complex series, which had caused great difficulty for previous students.

Memories of her work at Bletchley Park, Eastcote and Oakley were, of necessity, somewhat guarded. One interesting comment from Shaun Wylie, he being eighty-four at the time, surprisingly places Joan at GCHQ in 1958. There were a number of obituaries making reference to her work during the war:

> One of Joan Murray's important contributions to Hut 8's attack on naval *Enigma* accelerated the solution of *Offizier* signals, which were extremely difficult to break (some were never decoded), since they were re-enciphered with a second set of plugboard settings and a different message key. She also specialised in the subtleties of Banburismus, without which the breaking of naval *Enigma* would have been greatly slowed down, since *Bombes* were in very short supply until US Navy four-rotor *Bombes* came into service in August 1943. Following the decline of Banburismus in the summer of 1943, when it became ineffective after 'Dolphin' started to use the four-rotor machine, M4, she remained in Hut 8 as a highly capable member of a small team which broke navel ciphers until the end of the war.

> Joan Murray had an acute intelligence, which enabled her fully to hold her own with her male co-workers in Hut 8. She was also known as 'one of the really good cryptanalysts' in GCHQ. She was an enthusiastic and encouraging colleague, and much liked and admired by all who worked with her at BP and GCHQ.

> She served her country well, in a noble cause.

History has not treated Joan well. She was a woman in a man's world. She was not strident, nor was she meek. She was content to be judged on her abilities, but if her male superiors were unable to recognise her abilities, then it did not diminish them but simply clouded them from view. She deserved more but, living in an age before 'women's lib', she was a realist and being a realist meant that she made her contribution where she could rather than where she thought she was entitled.

Joan, at least in the early years, earned less than her male colleagues – even those less qualified and with less responsibility than her. In retrospect the unfairness of that is only too obvious, but she was not viewing the situation in retrospect and should not be judged as such. Neither should the men who were in charge, they also were of their time. A very real situation existed and Joan Clarke was instrumental in defeating Adolf Hitler and his 'wolf packs'. If she had stood firm on principles of 'equal pay for equal work' she may have been eventually successful – but in a Nazi governed Europe.

Some might say that Joan was presented with some form of immortality as a result of the 2014 film *The Imitation Game*, starring Benedict Cumberbatch playing the part of Alan Turing and Keira Knightley that of Joan Clarke, with some considerable artistic licence. Based on Andrew Hodges' book, the emotional aspects of the film, a minor part of his book, sealed Joan's fate, to be remembered simply as Turing's one time fiancé. Her contribution to the breaking of the naval *Enigma*, and her doggedness during the whole of the war, overlooked.

The little information available about Joan's private life points to her family as being an integral, but not a dominating, part of her life. The bond between Joan and Silvia lasted for the whole of their lives, and Silvia's connection to her brothers maintained by her frequent visits back to Britain; her last earlier in the year in which she died. Pat Goodland, in Canada, wrote to Martin Clarke shortly before Silvia's death:

> I don't know whether you know of me but Silvia lived with my family
> for many years when I was a child. She has told me that I am as close to
> a daughter as she has. We have a very special, close relationship. It is
> total, absolute, unconditional love. I have always looked up to Silvia as
> my model and I measure everyone I know against her. I am not the only

one who loves her so dearly. She has many, many fiends here. They are visiting her all the time. We are keeping her well supplied with flowers, ginger, sherry, martinis and gin and tonics. All with the doctors' approval! She has a room to herself which is just as well because the other patients would be jealous of all her visitors. So we are keeping a close watch over her.

I know she had a wonderful time in England, despite her illness. She remembered your party well and told us all about it. She was determined to be there and nothing would have stopped her. I have heard about you and your family for most of my life. I feel very close to you, even though we have never met. We will take good care of Silvia. She knows that this is her time to leave us. She is at peace with that. It looks like she will go peacefully and beautifully for she is sleeping a lot now. That's the way a beautiful lady should be allowed to go. God is looking out for her[74].

After Silvia's death, Martin wrote back to Pat Goodland in Canada:

Thank you so much for your letter. I shall cherish it. We here know how many good friends Silvia had in Canada, and that anything that could be done for her comfort and support would be done. I think now that I was too fainthearted in not going to her memorial service. I am eighty-six years old – eighty-five then - but I think I could have managed it.

I feel Silvia's loss more than you might expect when we lived so far apart. But particularly in more recent years I have valued her visits more; she and I often went off for a few days together to visit some place associated with the family or with an earlier visit; and since my wife's death she has come to stay with me here for a few days when over here. I had a few days with Silvia in London [Ontario] after an international classical conference in Philadelphia - when was it? late

1950's I should say. I stayed in your parent's house and I think you were there at the time[75].

Silvia's funeral, or memorial service, was an opportunity for Joan to finally meet Silvia's 'family' in Canada, and to realise the warmth of feeling there had been for Silvia in her adopted country. A year after Silvia's death Pat Goodland wrote to Joan and sent some mementoes of Silvia, including further examples of her art, painting being an ability for which she was generally praised. In Joan's reply there is a sense of resignation, yet it's quite clear that she was still fighting against her growing infirmity:

> That was rather a wonderful letter that you sent me. Of course I knew from Silvia that yours was a very special relationship, and it was obvious too when I met you at the service. I would have written before, but it was too late to expect to reach you for Christmas, so instead I concentrated on cards and letters for the UK, first. I can't do much at a time, because my right hand is almost useless - well, I've been writing my name, and typing with one hand where possible. I hope that an operation can be recommended.

> I wish I'd found out more about your job. I thought of you when an American came to interview me for a radio programme - Washington public service radio. She was about your age, and had obtained a grant to make a programme on the British intelligence contribution in World War II. This was last summer, VE time. She seemed very pleased - obviously rather a feminist, and pleased to have a variety of voices. But I was only one of a team, and feel I may have had too much attention recently, as a survivor and a woman, and because I worked on German naval, and the Atlantic convoys were so important.

> Silvia was very unlike me - I'm not an outgoing person, with such a multitude of friends. She used to make friends with children when we were both at school, and once had a fortune-teller saying she would have quite a family of her own. I fancy that wasn't a serious fortune-teller, but someone doing it at a church bazaar! And she should have

married. When she met my husband, when we too were staying in London (England), I remember thinking afterwards how much more attractive she was, and their ages were right - but I don't think I was really jealous.

However much we miss Silvia, we can't feel that death at her age is tragic, as for the much younger. And even more in the case of Jock's cousin's husband, who died in September, blind and bedridden, although still a great blow for his wife of more than fifty years, and childless.

Thank you for the offer of copies of my parent's wedding photo. You gave me the negative, of course. I don't know of anyone who would want a copy - brother Martin has the original, and Eileen thinks that we Clarkes of my generation do too much harping back, when we get together. I hear that you have written to both of them. But I would like to have the prayer book. We used to see quite a lot of my mother's parents, less of the other grandfather, who died earlier.

I am glad we have so many of Silvia's works. I now have two on my living room walls, and the calligraphy shown at the service, framed in my bedroom[76].

Eileen Clarke, the wife of Joan's brother Basil, in one of her letters to Pat Goodland, compared the two sisters as Joan, not at all easy to get to know, showing very little emotion except for her recent interest in numismatics, certainly not a person to whom you could easily talk on the phone. She described Silvia as being quite the opposite; "each time she came over to England we seemed to carry on as though there had never been a year's interval since we last met"[77].

Studio portrait of Silvia Clarke

(courtesy of Pat Goodland, Silvia's friend)

Joan's engagement to Alan Turing remains a puzzle. It might be possible to dismiss it as simply being fuelled by the intensity of the very special tasks they were undertaking together in a very rarified atmosphere; a sense of camaraderie being misinterpreted as love by two young people thrown together. Turing may have been attempting to conform to the pattern of behaviour, which he would have observed among the many couples that worked at Bletchley Park and formed romantic attachments. Both Turing

155

and Joan Clarke had been educated in an environment that, while not monastic, was not 'mixed' in the true sense of the word.

They both came from a background that put value upon the social circle in which they moved, and family connections were prized more highly than mere acquaintance. Joan was already known to Turing before their meeting at Bletchley Park, as Martin Clarke's sister, which meant that they were both seen as being within the same circle. Marriages were often between friends of a brother or sister, or close friends, or friends of friends. So, it might be thought, that Turing and Joan pre-qualified for a romantic attachment. The marriage of Joan's parents, William Clarke and Dorothy Fulford, led to marriage between William's brother Herbert and Dorothy's sister Phylis.

Joan's family appear to have been quite happy with the engagement but Turing's family, not so. His brother John was particularly offensive in his remarks, referring to Joan's unwashed hair and her personal hygiene; his mother Sara, in the biography of her son, does not even mention her. John Turing wrote of their absurd and farcical engagement, she an earnest female mathematician who might be described as extremely 'safe'.

> Alan's fiancée was tough going. We, parents and elder brother [John], worked like beavers all the weekend on this unpromising female and were exhausted by the exercise (as, no doubt, was she). I have an improbable memory of Alan and his affianced dutifully holding hands in a sandpit, both of them obviously wishing that they could get on with some untried theorem.
>
> The lady in question, it seems, was the only daughter of a country parson. If you are looking for a man who is after the money, give me one of those old-type country parsons . . . delicate hints about money and finally the firm proposal of a marriage settlement . . . he was fed up with the poor girl and we heard no more of her[78].

John Turing's reasons for being quite so scathing and unkind are not clear. If he did not know of his brother's homosexuality at the time of the engagement, he certainly did at the time that he penned the 'afterword' to his mother's book. He makes it quite clear that he did not like homosexuals and felt that it was intolerable that his brother should be identified as an early 'gay crusader'. His judgement of women appears to have been entirely based on looks and overt sexuality; the unattractive being termed 'safe' and the attractive as 'unsafe'.

John Turing seemed to have seen himself as one who was attracted to 'unsafe' women, claiming that his parents were well accustomed to his landing them with "young, attractive and lively young women with whom I fell in love at intervals of about six months at a time". Perhaps he was unable to accept that a Turing was drawn to the 'safe' Joan Clarke when he, entirely heterosexual, was secure with the 'unsafe'. He claimed that he hadn't the faintest notion that his brother was homosexual and that one did not (at least in the middle classes) talk or even think about homosexuals and lesbians.

When Joan did find love with Jock Murray their marriage lasted over thirty years and, by all indications, was a good marriage; she having the freedom to continue working with GCHQ during the most tense of times, he with GCHQ in a slightly less demanding role. They came together to share their common interest in numismatics, a field in which they both excelled, and one in which they could enjoy the limelight denied them at GCHQ.

FOOTNOTE

Since finishing writing the story of Joan Clarke the question of her time spent in Crail has remained a continuing puzzle. Nothing tangible remains in Crail but that her name, along with Jock's, does appear on the Register of Electors, and is the only testament to her ever having been there. Jock, as previously mentioned, had some involvement with the town but they appear, jointly, to have made very little impact.

When visiting Crail, on the coast of Fife, it's easy to see the attraction of living in that beautiful town. Nethergate although, as its name suggests, being the lower of the two roads running parallel to the Firth of Forth, sits high off the water. Priors Croft, standing next to a grand, but austere, row of granite villas, presents itself to Nethergate as a modest single story dwelling, but to the south hugs the falling land to present two stories to the sea. With the garden falling away to the south, Joan and Jock were rewarded with stunning views across to the Isle of May and, beyond that, to St Abb's Head in the far distance. Crail boasts a small, tight harbour where crabs and lobsters are still landed and, during Joan and Jock's years in the town, herring would have been plentiful during the 'season'.

Indirectly, Jock Murray did have some connection with the town, as an old Indian Army colleague had moved to Crail some time before he and Joan had got married. Lieut-Colonel Frederick George Ratcliffe had also spent the war in India and then returned to Britain upon the conclusion of hostilities. Ratcliffe had no family connection with Scotland, on either his father's or his mother's side; nor did his wife, as far as can be ascertained. The two ex-soldiers lived next to one another in Nethergate; Ratcliffe at the Priory, and Jock at Priors Croft.

One lady remembers the Ratcliffes and the Murrays during their time in Crail. Being a student at the time she did not have a great deal to do with them but she recalls that her parents often played bridge with one or other of the couples. Her father was the local GP and her parents were either invited to Nethergate, or their friends would visit them in their Market Gate house, which also served as the surgery. The two men, she described as jolly and friendly, but her overriding memory of Joan was that she would not stay when casual visitors called, preferring to slip away from the company rather than engage in the customary small talk.

Jock and Joan's wartime work and subsequent years at Eastcote were, of course, not subjects for conversation at the time. However, it was noted by this same lady that a number of outsiders moved into Crail over a short period of time, prior to the establishment of the Joint Services School for Linguists in 1954. What was remarked upon was that "they all seemed to know one another".

There appears a strong possibility that East Fife was becoming an outpost of GCHQ, hidden within the military establishment at Crail Airfield that had already been earmarked for the JSSL, which could act as cover for the presence of Russian speakers in the area. It's but a short step for GCHQ to provide on-site cryptology and translation of the radio intercepts as part of the anti-Soviet measures being established all along the east coast of Britain. Many of the Y-Stations were still in use, adapted for postwar technology, providing the famous, but misnamed, 'four minute warning'.

There is every chance that Joan and others, perhaps including Jock part time, were working indirectly for GCHQ. Certainly those ten years, between 1952 and 1962, do not appear in her pension calculations but government departments are not unable to bend the rules if it suits them. By the time of their return, GCHQ had moved to Cheltenham, where many of the earlier anti-Soviet measures had been taken over by the large mainframe computers.

Joan's return to GCHQ was extremely straightforward and simply executed. The remark by Shaun Wylie, of seeing Joan in Cheltenham during her lost years in Crail, is significant and must add credence to the possibility of Joan's early Cold War years. She was, without doubt, considered a major asset to GCHQ and this is borne out by her frequent visits to Washington during later years. It's possible that the years in Crail were a way of 'banking' that asset until Jock's health improved, or an alternative outcome permitted her return.

How GCHQ capitalised upon their asset remains a mystery. Joan was subject to the Official Secrets Act from the moment she signed the act in 1940, until she died. The little she felt able to say, when the very existence of GCHQ had only recently become known, was guarded and only to the extent that GCHQ was prepared to sanction. She took her responsibilities and promises seriously.

The picture painted of Joan was of a shy, even timid, woman. Writers have spoken of a stutter or other speech impediment; of being subservient to male colleagues and of deferring to them. The more accurate picture of Joan is that of a woman who was comfortable with her own intellect and did not feel the need to impress others in order to secure praise; instead she was quite content to be judged on her performance. Her speech was hesitant and cautious, but always with purpose; she had no need to impress, but was liked and admired by her colleagues.

My disappointment in examining the life of Joan Clarke: that she did not live to reach the age of one hundred, and give me the honour and pleasure of meeting her.

Anthony J Randall

Appendix A

Notable Persons

ALEXANDER, Hugh – born 19th April 1909 in Cork as Conel Hugh O'Donel Alexander. After his father died in 1920, the family moved to Birmingham, where he attended King Edward's School and then won a scholarship to King's College, Cambridge to study mathematics. He was British Chess Champion in 1938 and represented England in the Chess Olympiads four times during the 1930s. He joined Bletchley Park in February 1940 and worked in Hut 6, transferring to Hut 8 in 1941. After the war he worked for the company John Lewis, where he worked under Gordon Welchman, but returned to GCHQ, first at Eastcote then at Cheltenham. His continued interest in chess saw him again become British Chess Champion in 1956 and represent England in the Chess Olympiad twice more. His chess career was hampered by travel restrictions imposed because of his work for GCHQ. Towards the end of his life he was the chess columnist for *The Sunday Times*. He died 15th February 1974 in Cheltenham.

BATEY, Mavis Lilian (nee Lever) – born 5th May 1921 in Dulwich, attending Coloma Convent Girls' School in Croydon and then studying German at University College, London. Initially being employed to scan the personal columns in The Times for coded spy messages, she was then recruited to work for Dilly Knox in Hut 6 at Bletchley Park. She worked on breaking the Italian Naval Enigma code and worked on the Abwehr *Enigma* code. She married a fellow Bletchley Park mathematician, Keith Batey, in 1942 and continued with GCHQ for a short period after the war, following which she developed an interest in historical gardens, writing a number of books on that subject. She also wrote a biography of Dilly Knox *Dilly: The Man Who Broke Enigmas*. Batey was an active member of Campaign for the Protection of Rural England. She died 12th November 2013 at Petworth in Sussex.

BIRCH, Frank – born 5th December 1889 in London as Francis Lyall Birch, educated at Eton and then King's College, Cambridge, following which he lectured in history until leaving the academic life for the stage. At the outbreak of war he rejoined GC&CS at Bletchley Park, having been attached to Military Intelligence during the first war, and worked in the Naval Section, becoming its head in 1941. After the war he returned to acting, appearing in several films and television plays, before his death on 14th February 1956 at West Firle in Sussex.

BODSWORTH, Wilfred

CAIRNCROSS, John – born 25th July 1913 at Lesmahagow near Lanark in Scotland where he went to the local grammar school. He spent time at the University of Glasgow, the Sorbonne and then Trinity College, Cambridge, studying French and German. He then worked in the Cabinet Office as a private secretary and then joined the Foreign Office, transferring to Bletchley Park in 1942. He was a member of the Communist Party prior to the outbreak of war but not part of the Philby, Burgess, Maclean, Blunt group. During his time at Bletchley Park he was passing Tunny encrypts to the Soviets. By the end of the war he worked for the Treasury but confessed in 1952 to his previous activities and was dismissed although not prosecuted, moving first to the United States and then to Rome. The story finally came to public notice in 1963 when Philby defected to Moscow and Cairncross was named as the 'fifth man'. He moved from Rome to the south of France and then back to Britain where he married Gayle Brinkerhoff, an American opera singer. He died 8th October 1995 at his home in Hertfordshire.

CLARKE, Basil – born 6th March 1908 in Cambridgeshire as Basil Fulford Lowther Clarke, the eldest brother of Joan Clarke. He studied theology at St John's College, Durham, ordained in 1932, he then served as a curate before being appointed vicar at Knowl Hill in Berkshire. He married Eileen Coates in 1939. He is best known for his work on church architecture, visiting and documenting thousands of churches and cathedrals. Basil Clarke died 1978 and is buried at Knowl Hill in Berkshire.

CLARKE, Henry – born 23rd November 1850 at Firbank in Westmorland as Henry Lowther Clarke, and educated at Sedbergh School and then at St John's College, Cambridge and was ordained in 1874. In 1876 he married Alice Lovell Kemp and they had five children, their son William being the father of Joan Clarke. In 1903 he was appointed Bishop of Melbourne in Australia, and in 1905 Archbishop. He returned to England in 1920 to retire and died in 23rd June 1926, buried in Lymington, Hampshire.

CLARKE, Martin – born 2nd October 1909 in Suffolk as Martin Lowther Clarke, an elder brother of Joan Clarke. He was educated at Haileybury School in Hertfordshire and then King's College, Cambridge, and it was through Martin that his sister Joan was first introduced to Alan Turing. In the run up to the war he was first at Edinburgh and then at University College, London. During the war he worked at the Foreign Office, dealing with the affairs of Iceland and Faroes. After the war he was appointed Professor of Latin at Bangor. He died 29 May 2010.

CLARKE, Silvia – born 16th November 1911 at Cavendish in Suffolk as Silvia Mary Lowther Clarke, sister of Joan Clarke. She attended Dulwich High School for Girls, leaving school to work for the BBC. After the war she emigrated to Canada where she died October 1994.

CLARKE, Stephen – born 1914 at Cavendish in Suffolk as Stephen Kemp Lowther Clarke, brother of Joan Clarke. He died 6th March 1924,

CLARKE, William – born 16th December 1879 at Hedon in Yorkshire, not far from Hull, as William Kemp Lowther Clarke, known in the family as 'Kemp' rather than William. He was the father of Joan Clarke, and son of Henry. He attended Jesus College, Cambridge and was ordained in 1905. He was the secretary of the Society for the Promotion of Christian Knowledge for some years before joining Chichester Cathedral as a canon. He died 8th April 1968 at Chichester.

FLOWERS, Tommy – born 22nd December 1906 in Poplar, as Thomas Harold Flowers. After an apprenticeship in mechanical engineering he took a degree in electrical engineering and then joined the GPO and worked at their research station in Dollis Hill, London. During the war he helped Alan Turing in the development of the *Bombe* and later worked with Frank Morrell on *Colossus* to solve the *Lorenz* code. He never received appropriate recognition during his lifetime, dying 28th October 1998 in Mill Hill, London.

GOOD, Jack – born 9th December 1916 in London, as Isadore Jacob Gudak to Polish parents and attended the Haberdashers' Aske's Boys' School before studying mathematics at Jesus College, Cambridge. He joined Bletchley Park in 1941, working in Hut 8 on naval Enigma with Alan Turing, with whom he did not get on. Later he worked with the group that was developing *Colossus*. After the war he joined Turing at Manchester University, then returned to GCHQ at Eastcote. He went on to Trinity College, Oxford before moving to the USA in 1967 where he was appointed Professor at Virginia Tech, a position he held for some years, dying, unmarried, 5th April 2009 in Radford, Virginia.

HINSLEY, Harry – born 26th November 1918 in Walsall as Francis Harry Hinsley, educated at Queen Mary's Grammar School then winning a scholarship to St. John's College, Cambridge where he read history. He joined GC&CS at Bletchley Park early in the war, working in Hut 4 on traffic analysis. In 1943 he was seconded to the US Navy in Washington. After the war he edited the official history *British Intelligence in the Second World War*, to which Joan Murray (nee Clarke) made considerable contributions. He died 16th February 1998 in Cambridge.

HODGES, Andrew – born 1949 in London he is the author of *Alan Turing: The Enigma*, on which he consulted with Joan. The book was the basis of the film *The Imitation Game* directed by Morten Tyldum and starring Benedict Cumberbatch. A mathematician in his own right, Hodges has worked on twistor theory for many years.

KENDRICK, Tony

KNOX, Dillwyn – born 23rd July 1884 as Alfred Dillwyn Knox he went to Summer Fields School in Oxford, to Eton and then studied classics at King's College, Cambridge. During the first war he was a cryptanalyst in the Royal Navy and then with GC&CS liaising with French and Polish cryptanalysts on early investigations of *Enigma* and their development of *Bombes*. He worked at Bletchley Park until his death, in 1943, of lymphoma. He died 27th February 1943 at his home in Hughenden, Buckinghamshire.

MAHON, Patrick

McVITTIE, George Cunliffe – born 5th June 1904 in Smyrna, Turkey. He studied mathematics and physics at the University of Edinburgh and then at Christ's College, Cambridge. During the war he worked for the Meteorological Service at Bletchley Park, and after the war at the University of Illinois, later returning to Britain where he died 8th March 1988 in Canterbury.

MILNER-BARRY, Stuart – born 20th September 1906 in Hendon, as Philip Stuart Milner-Barry, he attended Cheltenham College and then won a scholarship to Trinity College, Cambridge. Like Hugh Alexander he played in the international Chess Olympiads of 1937 and 1939. He was recruited to Bletchley Park by Gordon Welchman, with whom he then worked in Hut 6. During his years at Bletchley Park he shared a billet with Welchman. After the war he joined the Treasury, where he stayed until retirement. In his later years he defended Welchman's reputation and campaigned for the preservation of Bletchley Park. He died 25th March 1995 at Lewisham.

MURRAY, Jock – born 29th June 1910 in Cheltenham as John Kenneth Ronald Murray. He was educated at Wellington School before attending Sandhurst and then serving in India. He worked for GC&CS during the war as a Russian linguist and then at Eastcote where he met Joan Clarke, marrying in 1952. He died 8th November 1986 in Cheltenham.

NOSKWITH, Rolf – born 19th June 1919 in Chemnitz as Rolf Noskovitch, son of eastern European parents who had set up a clothing manufacturing company in

Germany, before emigrating in 1932 to Ilkeston, Derbyshire. He was educated at Nottingham High School and then studied mathematics at Trinity College, Cambridge. He began working at Bletchley Park in 1941, assigned to Hut 8, working on naval *Enigma*. After the war he worked at the family textile company and died on 3rd January 2013.

PENDERED, Richard – born 26th September 1921 in Wellingborough as Richard Geoffrey Pendered, he was educated at Winchester and then read mathematics at Magdalene College, Cambridge. He began working at Bletchley Park in 1941, initially in Hut 6, before transferring to Hut 8. He died 19th December 2010.

REJEWSKI, Marian – born 16th August 1905 in Bydgoszcz, Poland and studied mathematics at Poznań University, then working on cryptology on a clandestine course run by the Polish Cipher Bureau. He developed a machine to assist in breaking the commercial version of *Enigma*, without a plugboard. At the outbreak of war he and some of his colleagues escaped to France to continue their work and then, when France was overrun, to England. After the war he returned to work in Poland, where he died 13th February 1980 in Warsaw.

ROCK, Margaret – born 7th July 1903 in Hammersmith, passed the London General School Exam going to Bedford College, London, and then worked as a statistician in industry. Her father had died during the first war when HMS *Laurentic* sank off the coast of Ireland. At Bletchley Park she worked for Dillwyn Knox, alongside Margaret Batey nee Lever. After the war she continued for some years with GCHQ, dying 26th August 1983 in Worcester.

STEWART, Bernard Harold Ian Halley – born 10th August 1935 was a leading member of the British Numismatic Society where he became acquainted with and a friend of Joan and Jock. He was the member of Parliament for Hitchin, Hertfordshire and raised to the peerage in 1991 where he sat in the House of Lords as Baron Stewartby, of Portmoak. He wrote obituaries for both Jock and Joan on their deaths.

STRIPP, Alan – born 17th October 1924 he was a classics scholar at Trinity College, Cambridge and joined Bletchley Park in 1944 to translate intercepted signals from the Japanese Air Force. In 1944 he was posted to the Wireless Experimental Centre at Delhi where Jock Murray was stationed. At the end of the war he was transferred to Rawalpindi on the North West Frontier, where he took a crash course in Farsi and, after that he returned to Cambridge. He died 18th March 2009 in Linton, Cambridgeshire

TILTMAN, John – born 25th May 1894 in London, of Scottish parents, as John Hessell Tiltman. He served as a cryptanalyst with the Indian Army in Simla returning to work at GC&CS in the build-up to war. Although he did not have a university education he was considered to have made a significant contribution to the code breaking at Bletchley Park. After the war he continued to work for GCHQ, being appointed Assistant Director. He died 10th August 1982 in Hawaii.

TRAVIS, Edward – born 24th September 1888 in Blackheath, London, as Edward Wilfred Harry Travis. He joined the Royal Navy in 1906 where he worked on navy ciphers. He worked for GC&CS, transferring to Bletchley Park at the outbreak of war, and became deputy director in 1942.

TURING, Alan Mathison – born 23rd June 1912 in Maida Vale, London as Alan Mathison Turing. Educated at Hazelhurst Preparatory School in Frant then Sherborne School. He studied first at King's College, Cambridge and then at Princeton University where he met Shaun Wylie, and then returned to Cambridge as war was approaching and began working with GC&CS at Bletchley Park. He headed up Hut 8, responsible for breaking the naval *Enigma* and made further developments to the Polish *Bombe*. At the end of the war he continued to work on the concept and implementation of the electronic digital computer in London and Manchester. He was homosexual and was prosecuted and sentenced to a chemical based treatment which led eventually to his death on 7th June 1954 in Wilmslow, Cheshire.

TUTTE, Bill – born 14th May 1917 in Newmarket as William Thomas Tutte, he attended the Cambridge and County High School for Boys and then won a scholarship to study natural sciences at Trinity College, Cambridge. He joined Bletchley Park early in the war and worked on the Italian naval cipher, *Hagelin*. He transferred to working on the *Lorenz* project as part of the Research Section and wrote many of the algorithms used on *Colossus* to break the *Lorenz* code. After the war Tutte returned to Cambridge to complete his doctorate., then moved to Canada to work at the universities of Toronto and Waterloo. He retired to Kitchener in Ontario in 1995, where he died 2nd May 2002.

TWINN, Peter – born 9th January 1916 in Streatham as Peter Frank George Twinn, educated at Manchester Grammar School, Dulwich College and then Brasenose College, Oxford. He was the first mathematician recruited to Bletchley Park just before the outbreak of war, where he was first an assistant to Dillwyn Knox. He was already established as one of the Seniors in Hut 8 when Joan joined in 1940. After the war he did not continue with GCHQ but worked in various government departments including the Royal Aircraft Establishment in Farnborough and the Natural Environment Research Council. He died 29th October 2004.

WELCHMAN, Gordon – born 15th June 1906 in Bristol, he attended Marlborough College and then studied mathematics at Trinity and Sidney Sussex Colleges, Cambridge where he supervised Joan in geometry and later recruited her to join him at Bletchley Park. During the war he was head of Hut 6, working on the army and air force *Enigmas*. After the war he went into industry, then moved to the USA to work for various companies. He took American citizenship in 1962, dying 8th October 1985 in Newburyport, Massachusetts.

WYLIE, Shaun – born 17th January 1913 in Oxford, educated at the Dragon School, and then Winchester College where he won a scholarship to New College, Oxford where he studied both mathematics and classics. He spent some time at Princeton University in New Jersey, where he met Alan Turing, after becoming a fellow at Trinity College, Cambridge. At Bletchley Park he was the head of the crib sub-section in Hut 8, transferring in 1943 to work on the *Lorenz* code. In 1958, while Joan was in Scotland, he was made Chief Mathematician at GCHQ and was there to welcome her return in 1962.

YOXALL, Leslie – born 18th May 1914 in Salford as Albert Leslie Yoxall, was educated at Manchester Grammar School and Sidney Sussex College, Cambridge. He was recruited, by Gordon Welchman, from a teaching position at his old school to join Hut 8 to work with Joan on breaking the *Offizier* code, later moving to Hut 7 to work on the Japanese naval cipher. After the war he continued with GCHQ, later working as a liaison officer in Washington. He died 30th September 2005.

APPENDIX B

SELECTED DOCUMENTS

GOVERNMENT COMMUNICATIONS
HEADQUARTERS
Room No. E/0605
Oakley, Priors Road, CHELTENHAM, Glos.
Telephone: Cheltenham 55321, ext. 2074

Your reference:
G.C.H.Q. reference: H/5312/P

16th January, 1962

Dear Murray,

    Boddy showed me your letter from which I am very
pleased to see that you are now a great deal better in
health - and it is this that prompts this letter. Is there
any chance (question expecting the answer no but hoping for
yes) that you and Joan would like to come back here if only
for a few years? If there were I would see whether we could
get round staff side difficulties (I think there is a good
chance that we could) and make you a decent offer. You
would both be very valuable to us - there is a lot to do on
Boddy's side and he would be delighted to have you back and
Shaun Wylie is equally enthusiastic about having Joan. Work
here I would say is generally more varied and interesting in
H than when you both left. I very much hope that - unless
health considerations rule it out - you will consider this
seriously.

2.   The 'staff side' problem mentioned above is the
difficulty of bringing people in anywhere except at the
bottom of the ladder; I think however that the argument on
the basis of special qualifications would be so strong in
your case that we should be able to manage it.

3.   Best wishes to you both; Shaun who brightened visibly
at the possibility of Joan's return - sends the same.

Yours very sincerely

Hugh Alexander

Lt. Col. J. K. R. Murray,
Priorscroft,
Nethergate,
Crail, Fife.

Leave Crail 13th Tues.
an cheek 14th

**GOVERNMENT COMMUNICATIONS
HEADQUARTERS**
Room No. E/0605
Oakley, Priors Road, CHELTENHAM, Glos.
Telephone: Cheltenham 55321, ext. 2074

Your reference:
G.C.H.Q. reference: H/5424/P   26th January, 1962

Dear Toch,

I hope the enclosures sent with this letter won't
immediately put a damper on any wishes you might have to return!
Unfortunately in order for us to be able to bring you up to date
with work here, we have to go through the tiresome business of
vetting and, nine years having passed, we cannot avoid it.

2.   However the Security Division think they can get the whole
tiresome business through very quickly: if you could give a
couple of referees, other than GCHQ people - up in your present
part of the world would probably be best, because obviously it
is the last nine years that they have to cover - Security will
send a chap up immediately to Scotland and dispose of the affair.
If you could send the forms back by return post then the
Security chap will come down in week February 5th/9th - and I
hope that you might both come down perhaps about February 14th
and visit the office on February 15th and/or February 16th.
Then we shall be able to talk freely.

3.   Very much looking forward to seeing you both.

Yours

Hugh Alexander

Lt. Col. J. K. R. Murray,
Priorscroft,
Nethergate,
Crail, Fife.

I see that I haven't said how
delighted we all were with your interest in returning
— that can be taken for granted. Also I think (we can
discuss this) that 'probation' period could be arranged.

01-286-2084

67 Lauderdale Mansions,
Lauderdale Road,
London W.9.
7 December 1977

Dear Mrs Murray,

I am writing to you on a very delicate matter.
I have been commissioned by Andre Deutsch the publishers
to write a biography of Alan Turing. Your friendship
with him in 1941 has been described to me by several
people, and Shaun Wylie was kind enough to give me
your address.

Perhaps you might like to think about what you
would be willing to have said. There seem to me to be
a number of choices that could be made.

I might say that even if you wished to exclude
emotional matters from the account, I would still think
it important for me to mention you as one of his
colleagues. Particularly so as it would be a pity to
give the false impression that mathematics and cryptanalysis
were entirely male preserves.

There are a number of different issues involved
in all this, and from my point of view it would be
easiest if I had a chance to discuss them with you
personally - perhaps in the New Year. Could you let
me know how you feel?

I might mention that I am combining this project
with my research assistantship at Oxford, where I work
with Roger Penrose in the Maths. Institute.

Yours sincerely,

Andrew P. Hodges, Ph.D.

Use my maiden name only. ✓

Turing's contribution ~~[struck through]~~

Enigma. Welchman gave him most of the credit for the logical design of the Bombes, which was an enormous improvement ~~on~~ over the original Polish bombe. Also, how to use it on ~~a~~ related problems other forms of Enigma, e.g. ~~x~~. ~~without the~~ plugboard.
He was responsible for all the initial work on German naval Enigma usage (after a change which baffled the Poles), when others were concentrating on usage by the other services, which looked more promising.

General. Application of Bayes' theorem, for weighing the evidence. He developed independently some ideas which I believe were original, appear in formation although found in my later publications. He ~~they~~, ~~but~~, probably never considered what he did here as real mathematics, to be written up as such. (cf. See Turing p. 89) What mattered then was that it contributed ~~at that time~~ to the work of GC&CS. An example — his 'bloody little book' (not pejorative — it genuinely was ~~lit was actually a~~ somewhat bloodstained) provided a table of figures for assessing the significance of certain statistics. The basis was, I suppose, a compound Poisson distribution. He later explained verbally to Jack Good most of what he had done, and ~~&~~ Good wrote up the theory, including (I think) a satisfactory explanation of a correction term, whose ~~which~~ Turing had forgotten how it had arisen. ~~to the~~ Turing would explain probability matters in terms of taking balls out of urns, not refer one to a standard distribution.

[the permanent bonus]

After he left Hut 8 (or rather was still there physically, but working on possible applications of similar ideas for other parts of GC&CS)

[rows of typed ●●● symbols]

Joan's reply to Andrew Hodges' first draft – note that she is using pre-used sprocket fed computer paper, no doubt from GCHQ.

From the Director, Sir Brian Tovey KCMG

GOVERNMENT COMMUNICATIONS HEADQUARTERS
OAKLEY, CHELTENHAM, GLOS., GL52 5AJ
Telephone: Cheltenham 21491 ext.

D/3783DQ/1105/7

2 July 1982

Mrs J E L Murray
c/o DAO/H
E/0804
OAKLEY

Dear Joan,

    I understand that when you retired on 30 June
you had completed more than 20 years since you
rejoined GCHQ in 1962.

    Your service in our organisation does in total,
however, span much more than a mere twenty years, and
your contribution - primarily in the H field - has
been of great value and significance. May I accordingly
take this opportunity of thanking you for all that you
have done for us, and wish you many years of good health
and happiness in your retirement.

Yours sincerely,

Brian J M Tovey

**Oxford
University
Press**

Arts and Reference Division
Managing Director Ivon Asquith

Walton Street, Oxford OX2 6DP
Telephone 0865 56767
Telefax 0865 56646
Telex 837330 OXPRES G

7th June 1993

Joan Murray
7 Larkfields
Headington
Oxford
OX3 8PF

Dear Ms Murray

We have decided that we would like to celebrate the publication
of <u>Codebreakers: The Inside Story of Bletchley Park</u> with a small
reception at the Imperial War Museum and do hope that you will
be able to attend.

We will hold the reception on Thursday 26 August (the day on
which we hope to publish the book) at 12 pm and will be offering
wine and canapes.

There is a good cafe at the Imperial War Museum at which you
will be able to find a light lunch after the reception.

We hope to attract some interest from the media which may result
in diary pieces or short features in the national press. We
will have the Imperial War Museum's Enigma machine at the
reception so I am hoping that there will be demand for a
photograph or two.

We will be sending out official invitations at the end of July
but as you, the contributors, will be our most important guests
I would be very grateful if you could let me know whether you
think you will be able to attend and whether you will be
bringing a guest. I do not need a firm commitment at this stage
but would like to get a general idea of numbers and also wanted
to give you advance warning.

I realise that travelling to London for the day may be
inconvenient or difficult to arrange but I do hope that you will
be able to come.

Yours sincerely

Julia Dingle
Promotion Manager
(Humanities)

APPENDIX C

FAMILY PHOTOGRAPHS

Jock and Joan's marriage 1952

(courtesy of John Clarke, Joan's nephew)

Dorothy and Basil, Joan's mother and brother in Vicar's Close Chichester, date 1963

(courtesy of John Clarke, Joan's nephew)

Joan, thought to be in the late 1940s

(courtesy of John Clarke, Joan's nephew)

Jock and Joan's marriage 1952

(courtesy of John Clarke, Joan's nephew)

OTHER PHOTOGRAPHS

The walk from Vicar's Close into Chichester Cathedral taken by Joan at her marriage to Jock, and by the family at the funeral of her father William.
(author's photograph)

View from cottage in Crail, across the Firth of Forth
(author's photograph)

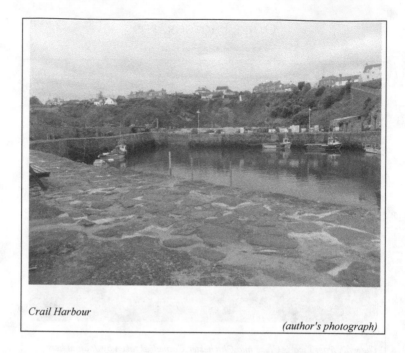

Crail Harbour

(author's photograph)

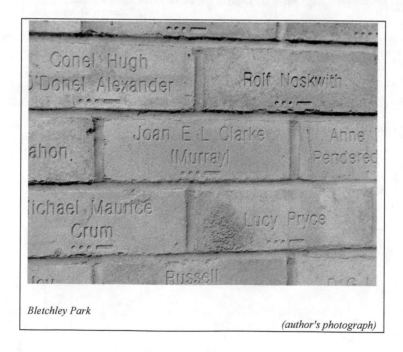

Bletchley Park

(author's photograph)

REFERENCES

1   Alexander Philip Kidd, The Brisbane Episcopate of St Clair Donaldson, 1996 University of Queensland

2   Randall Nolan, The Anglican Vocation in Australian Society, 2007 Griffith University, Brisbane

3   Laurie Lee, Cider with Rosie, 1959 Penguin Books

4   Joan Grigsby, This was Lymington, Paul Cave Publications

5   The Register (Adelaide South Australia), Monday 18th September 1922

6   J A H Brincker, Epidemiological and Etiological Study of Measles, 1938 Royal Society of Medicine

7   William Clarke – private papers

8   William Clarke – private papers

9   Nigel Graddon, The Mystery of U-33: Hitler's Secret Envoy, 2010 Adventures Unlimited Press

10   Nicholas Rankin, Ian Fleming's Commandos, 2011 Oxford University Press

11   German records show that the boat was the Schiff 26 (erroneously identified as the VP2623 in some accounts) B. Jack. Copeland, The Essential Turing, 2004 Oxford University Press

12   F H Hinsley, British Intellegence in the Second World War, 1981 HMSO

13   Hugh Alexander, quoted by Lindsey Ann Lord, University of St Andrews honours project

14   FH Hinsley & Alan Stripp, Code Breakers, The Inside Story of Bletchley Park (Joan Murray contribution), 1993 Oxford University Press

15   B. Jack. Copeland, The Essential Turing, 2004 Oxford University Press

16   Memorandum dated 20 October 1940 from Frank Birch, head of the naval interpretation section at Bletchley Park, to the Admiralty

17   David J. Sherman, The First Americans, 2016 National Security Agency

18   Hugh Sebag-Montefiore, Enigma, The Battle for the Code, 2000 Weidenfeld & Nicholson

19   American Mathematical Society Volume 64, Number 3

20   Andrew Hodges, Alan Turing: The Enigma, 1983 Burnett Books

21   Nicholas Rankin, Ian Fleming's Commandos, 2011 Oxford University Press

22   Nigel West, Historical Dictionary of Naval Intelligence, 2010 Scarecrow
        Press Inc.

23   Hugh Sebag-Montefiore, Enigma, The Battle for the Code, 2000 Weidenfeld
        & Nicholson. The author attributes the anecdote to Pauline Elliot, who
        worked in Hut 8, given to the author in an 1998-9 interview.

24   Hugh Sebag-Montefiore, Enigma, The Battle for the Code, 2000 Weidenfeld
        & Nicholson. The author attributes the anecdote to Baroness Jean
        Trumpington who as Jean Campbell Harris worked at Bletchley Park as a
        typist.

25   Nicholas Rankin, Ian Fleming's Commandos, Faber and Faber, 2011

26   Gordon Connell's report on the incident quoted by Hugh Sebag-Montefiore,
        Enigma, The Battle for the Code, 2000 Weidenfeld & Nicholson

27   Linda Monckton, 'Bletchley Park' (English Heritage, Architectural
        Investigation Reports and Papers B/010/2004, 2004), 3 vols., esp. 398-442.

28   Michael Smith, The Secrets of Station X, 2011 Biteback Publishing Ltd

29   Hugh Alexander, Cryptographic History of Work on German Naval Enigma,
        1945 Imperial Defence College

30   Hugh Sebag-Montefiore, Enigma, The Battle for the Code, 2000 Weidenfeld
        & Nicholson.

31   John Ross, The Forecast for D-Day, 2014, Lyons Press

32   John Ross, The Forecast for D-Day, 2014, Lyons Press

33   Sinclair McKay, The Secret Life of Bletchley Park, 2010 Aurum Press,
        London

34   Sinclair McKay, The Secret Listeners, 2012 Aurum Press

35   Hugh Sebag-Montefiore, Enigma, The Battle for the Code, 2000 Weidenfeld
        & Nicholson

36   Sir Edward Wilfred Harry Travis, Operational Head of Bletchley Park

37   Joss Pearson, Bletchley Park's Secret Room, 2011 Amberley Publishing

38   Patrick Mahon, The History of Hut 8, 2007 Graham Ellsbury

39   Sinclair McKay, The Secret Life of Bletchley Park, 2010 Aurum Press, London

40   Michael Smith, The Debs of Bletchley Park, 2015 Aurum Press, London

41   Edward Travis quoted by Richard J Aldrich, GCHQ, 2010 Harper Press

42   Sinclair McKay, The Spies of Winter, 2016 Aurum Press

43   Richard J Aldrich, GCHQ, 2010 Harper Press

44   Sinclair McKay, The Spies of Winter, 2016 Aurum Press

45   Unpublished private family papers

46   Unpublished private family papers (Letter to Henry Tropp)

47   Unpublished private family papers

48   BBC Horizon, The Strange Life and Death of Dr Turing, 1992, Director: Christopher Sykes

49   Family reminiscences

50   Andrew Hodges, Alan Turing: The Enigma, 1983 Burnett Books

51   Andrew Hodges, Alan Turing: The Enigma, 1983, Burnett Books Ltd

52   Chichester and Southdown Observer, 2nd August 1952

53   Andrew Hadfield, Art, Literature and Religion in Early Modern Sussex, 2014 Routledge

54   Unpublished private family papers

55   John Murray, A Crail Scrapbook, 2010 Crail Museum Trust

56   JKR Murray, The Numismatic Chronicle, 1968 (Vol. 37)

57   JKR Murray, The Numismatic Chronicle, 1969 (Vol. 38)

58   JKR Murray, The Numismatic Chronicle, 1970 (Vol. 39)

59   JEL Murray, The Numismatic Chronicle, 1971 (Vol. 40)

60   JKR Murray and BHIH Stewart, The Numismatic Chronicle, 1972 (Vol. 41)

61   JEL Murray, The Numismatic Chronicle, 1978 (Vol. 48)

62   JEL and JKR Murray, The Numismatic Chronicle, 1980 (Vol. 50)

63   DH Caldwell, JEL Murray and M.Delme-Radc, The Numismatic Chronicle, 1982 (Vol. 52)

64   JEL Murray, The Numismatic Chronicle, 1987 (Vol. 57)

65   Chichester and Southdown Observer, 26th April 1968

66   Julie Patenaude, Church of England's Church Buildings Division

67   Lord Stewartby, Obituary of Mrs J E L Murray, 1996 British Numismatic Society

68   Patricia Goodland, private letter to the author, 2019

69   James Stewart Reaney, The London Free Press, revised 2015

70   Unpublished private family papers

71   Unpublished private family papers

72   Unpublished private family papers

73   Unpublished private family papers

74   Pat Goodland, London Ontario – private papers

75   Pat Goodland, London Ontario – private papers

76   Pat Goodland, London Ontario – private papers

77   Pat Goodland, London Ontario – private papers

78   Sara Turing, Alan M Turing – Centenary Edition, 1959 & 2012 Cambridge University Press. Taken from John Turing's 'afterword'

79   JEL Murray, The Numismatic Chronicle, 1971 (Vol. 40)

INDEX